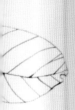

At Home with Handmade Books

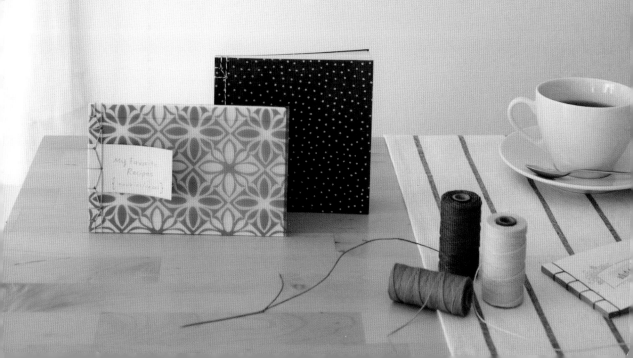

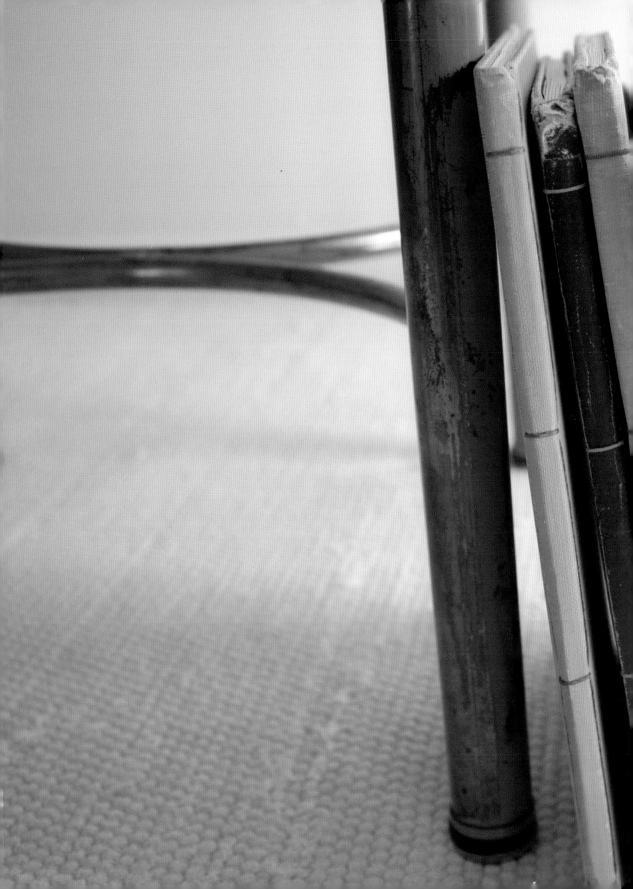

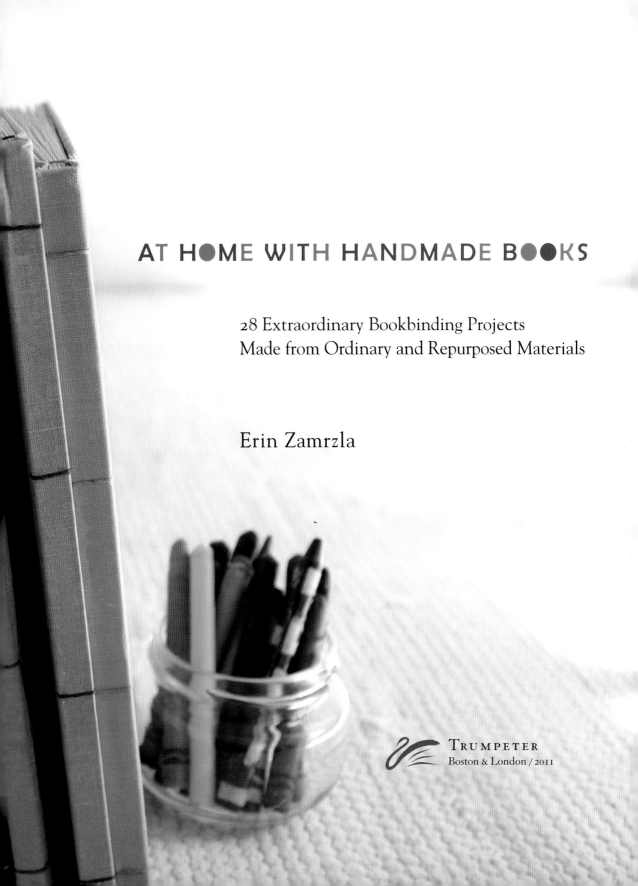

AT HOME WITH HANDMADE BOOKS

28 Extraordinary Bookbinding Projects
Made from Ordinary and Repurposed Materials

Erin Zamrzla

TRUMPETER
Boston & London / 2011

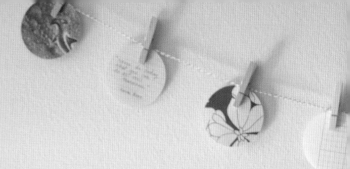

CONTENTS

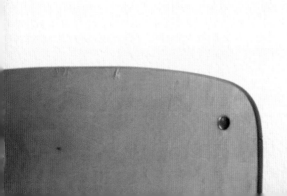

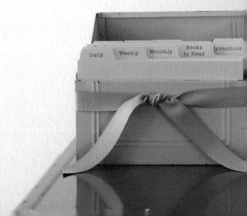

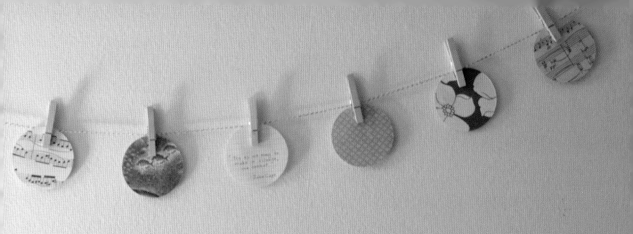

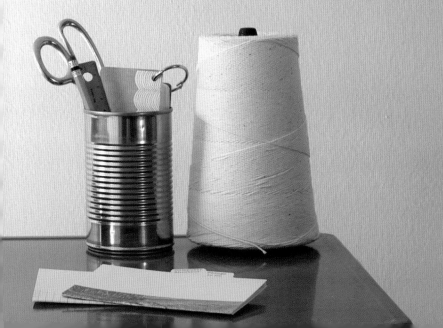

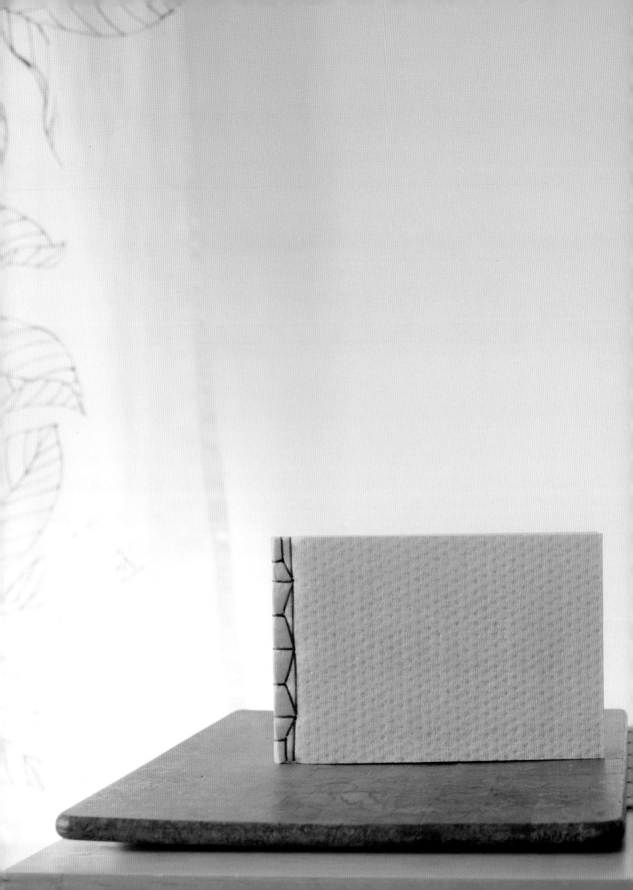

INTRODUCTION

I love to work with paper, create from scratch, and transform old things into something new and interesting. As an artist, I also sketch, draw, and jot down ideas on the go. Bookbinding is the perfect combination of these interests. I make books to use as sketchbooks and journals for myself and for others and must carry a handmade notebook with me at all times. I enjoy the beauty of the papers and bindings as well as the simplicity of an art form that extends back hundreds of years.

The projects in this book are adapted from traditional Japanese bindings for use with modern materials and purposes. I encourage you to make creative use of easy-to-find supplies that you may already have around the house. The different projects provide fun ways for you to journal, jot notes, make lists, doodle, draw, and display photos. Many of the completed projects make great gifts as well.

I hope that you fall in love with paper and its possibilities as you create these fun and functional projects.

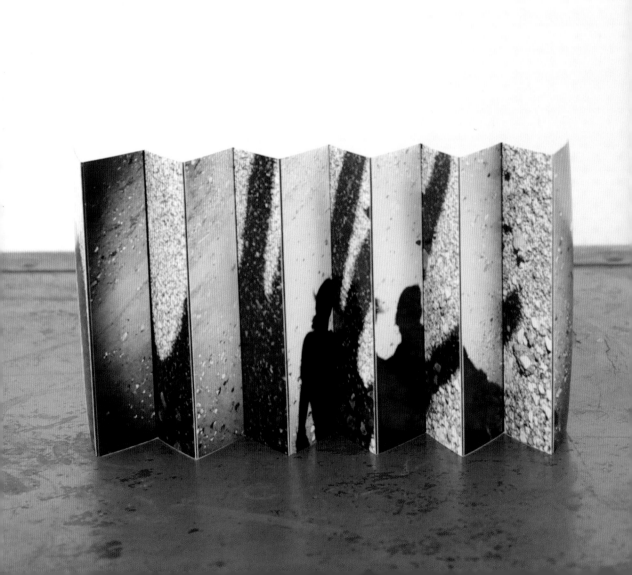

ACCORDION BOOKS

A basic accordion book is made by taking a long strip of paper and folding it back and forth, concertina style, until it is just the right size to fit inside the cover. Often, to get a strip of paper long enough, sheets of paper are pasted together end to end. As a variation, you can also begin with sheets of paper twice the width of your cover. When you fold each sheet in half and paste them together along their fore edges, you will end up with another traditional style of accordion book called an accordion album.

The accordion structure allows for fun variations and interesting ways to present your projects. Many of these books can stand up on their own when their pages are left partially unfolded, making them interesting displays.

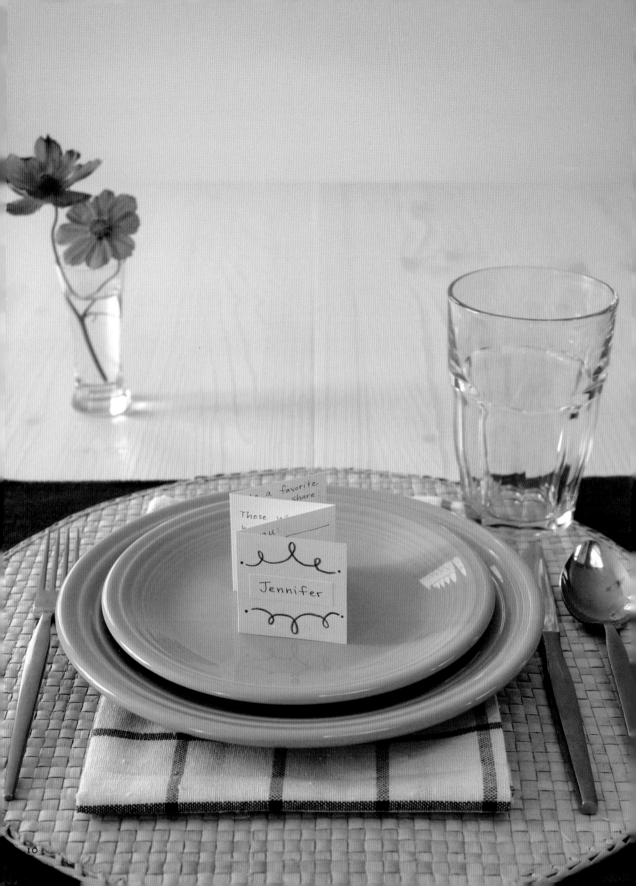

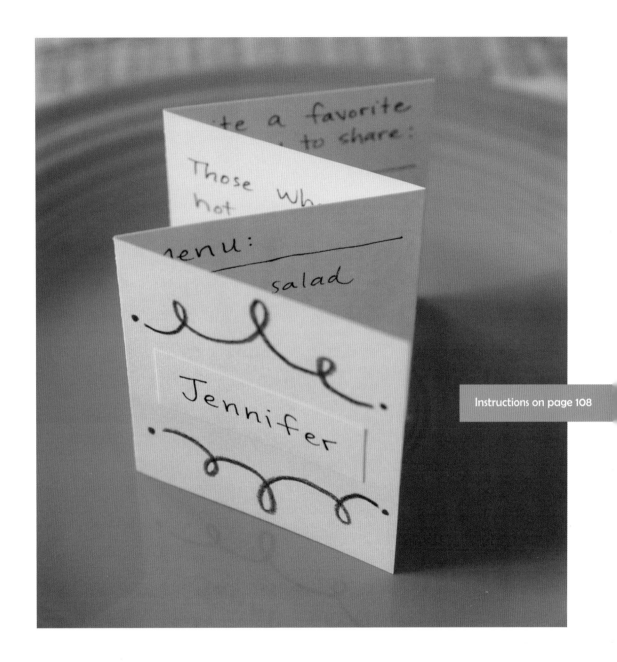

Instructions on page 108

BON APPÉTIT PLACE CARD

Display the names of your dinner guests with this basic accordion. It includes room for the menu, inspiring quotes, and other fun information, such as signatures from other guests.

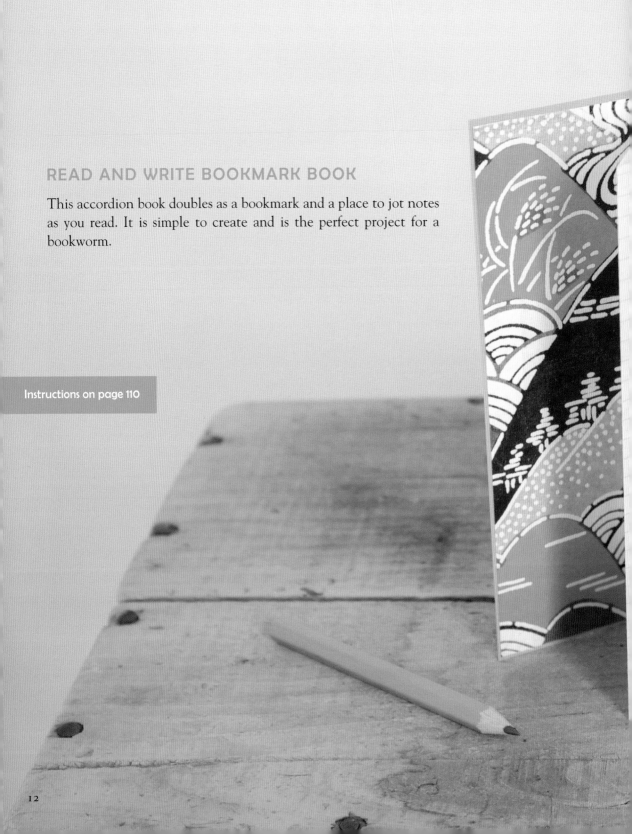

READ AND WRITE BOOKMARK BOOK

This accordion book doubles as a bookmark and a place to jot notes as you read. It is simple to create and is the perfect project for a bookworm.

Instructions on page 110

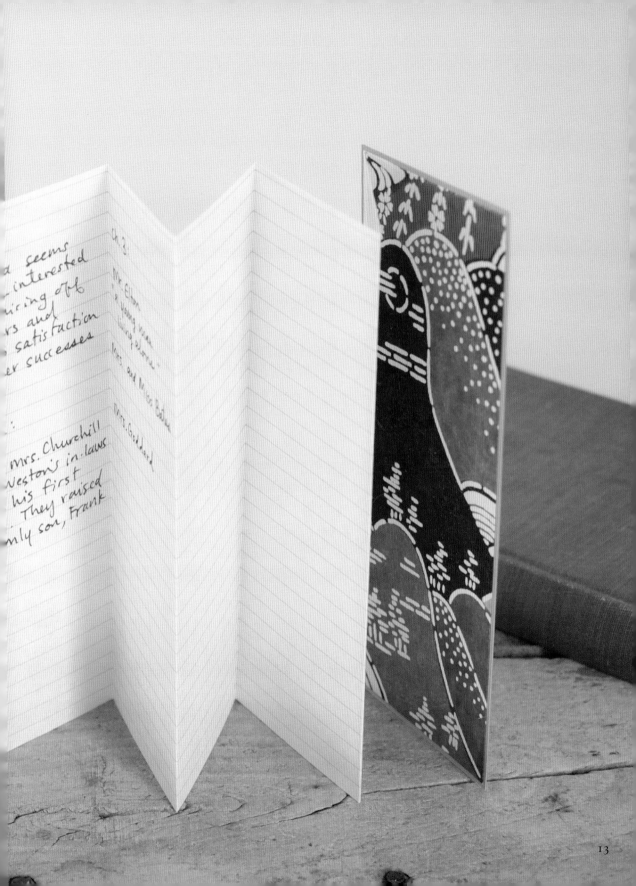

TWO- OR THREE-VIEW PICTURE

Look at this picture from one angle to see one image; look at it from another angle to see a different image. It's almost magic! Use two photos to create the two-view picture or use three photos to create the three-view picture.

Instructions on page 112

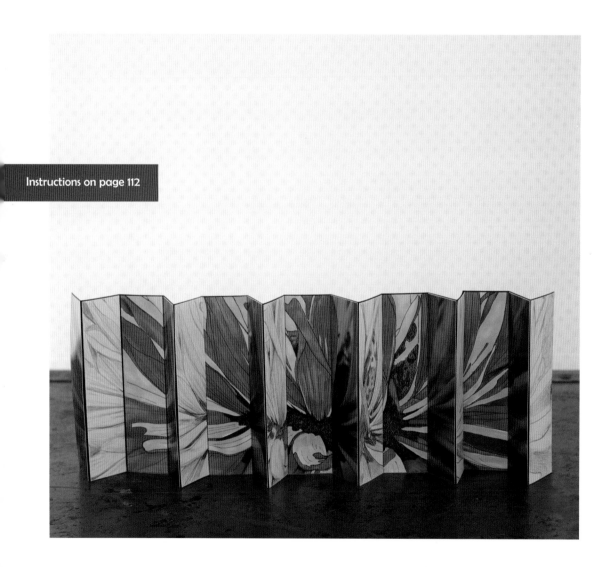

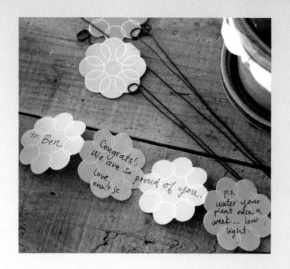

UNFOLDING FLOWER NOTES

This little book opens into a string of flowers, just like paper dolls. Use one of these accordion books as a note to accompany the gift of a plant. Instructions for making a wire floral pick are included.

Instructions on page 114

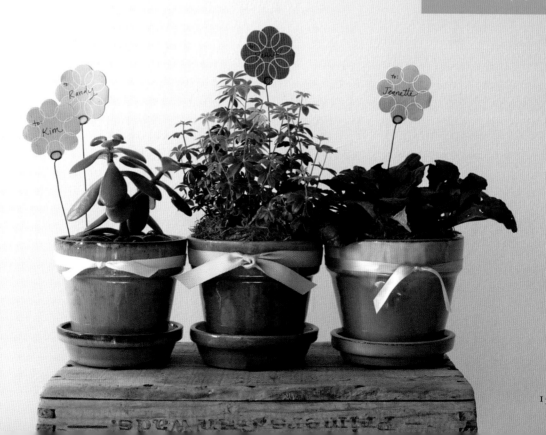

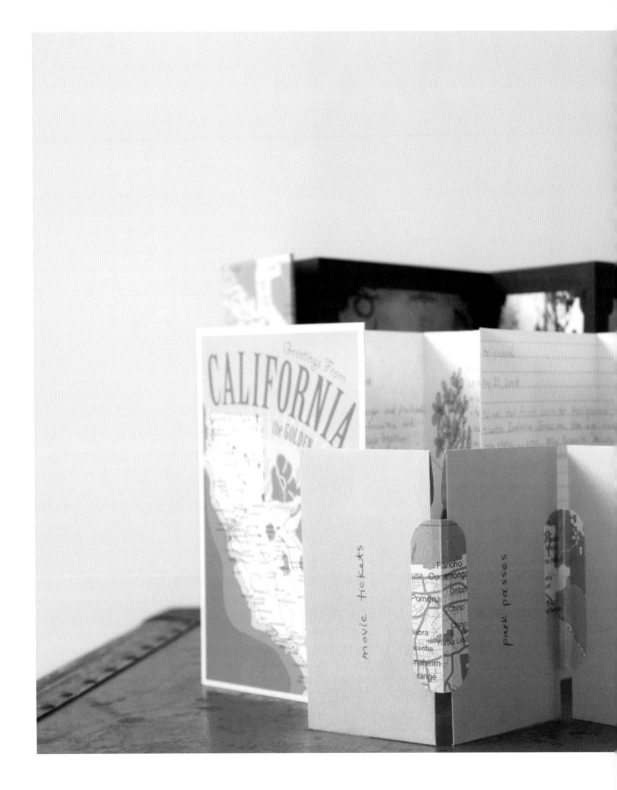

TRAVEL SET

Remember a favorite trip with this set of three accordion albums. Use one as a journal, another as a photo album, and a third to collect keepsakes from your travels. Instructions on pages 116–23.

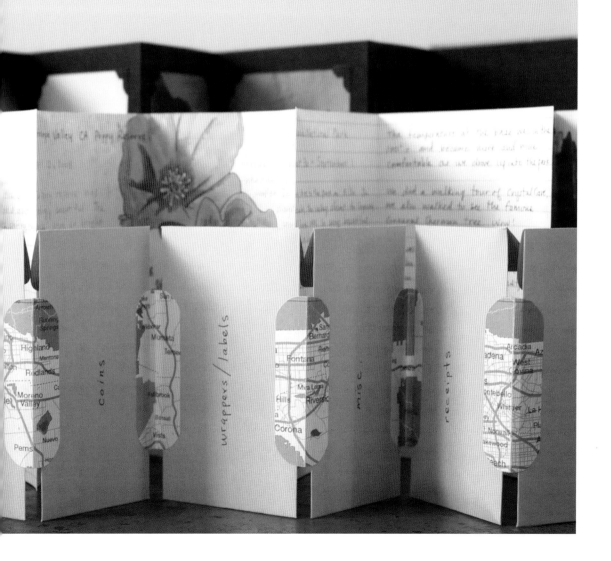

WISH-YOU-WERE-HERE POSTCARD JOURNAL

Jot down notes and sketches in this small journal as you travel. Postcards from your trip serve as the covers and ruled and blank pages fill the inside.

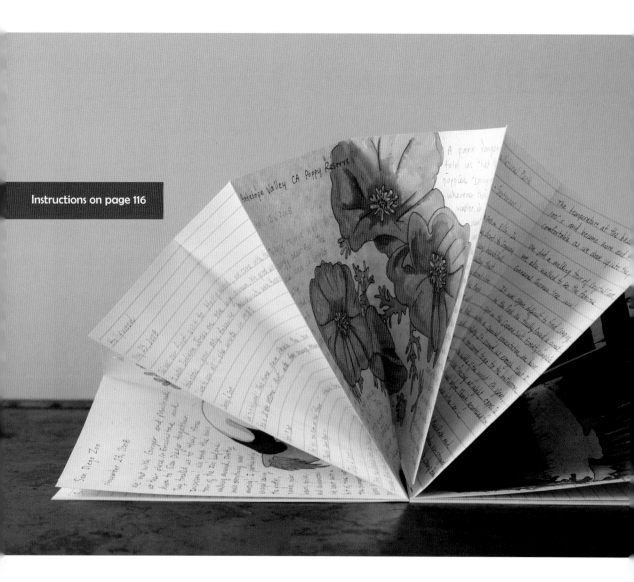

Instructions on page 116

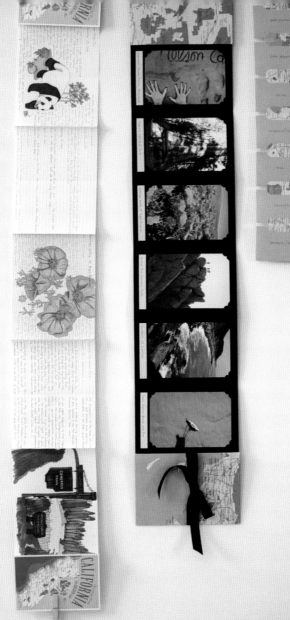

Instructions on page 118

TRAVEL PHOTO ALBUM

Keep a selection of favorite trip photos handy to share with others. Use a map or paper from your trip for the covers. Photo corners hold the pictures in place, and a ribbon keeps the book closed. You can even display the book standing open on a shelf—just tie the ribbon to the back, out of the way.

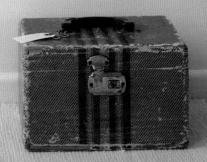

TINY SOUVENIR BOOK

Collect memories on the go and keep them in the pages of this tiny accordion.
The envelope pages hold tickets, notes, currency, and other small mementos.
A rubber band secures the closed book.

Instructions on page 122

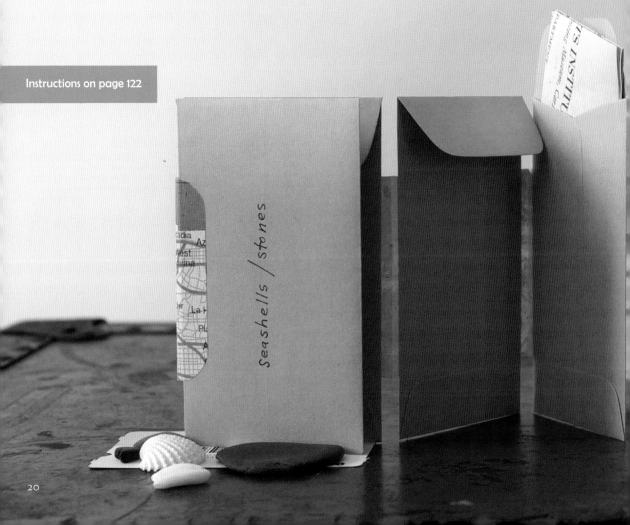

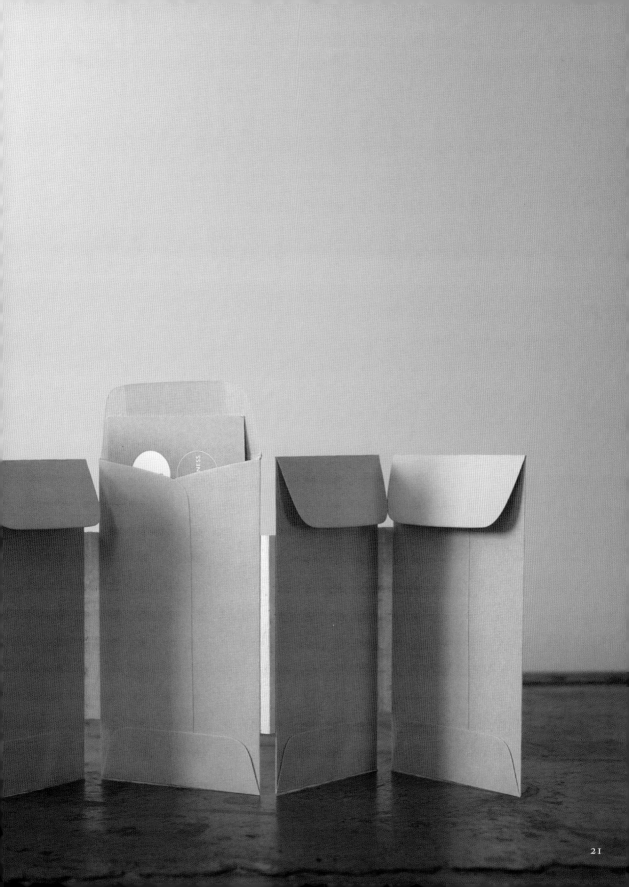

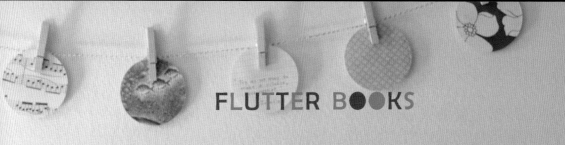

FLUTTER BOOKS

The only difference between a flutter book and an accordion book is the design of the cover; the cover of a flutter book is constructed of one piece and wraps around the spine. Pages are folded in accordion fashion and attached to the inside of both the front and the back of the cover.

As the pages are not connected at the spine, they can flutter out of the cover in a breeze. This is how the book received its name.

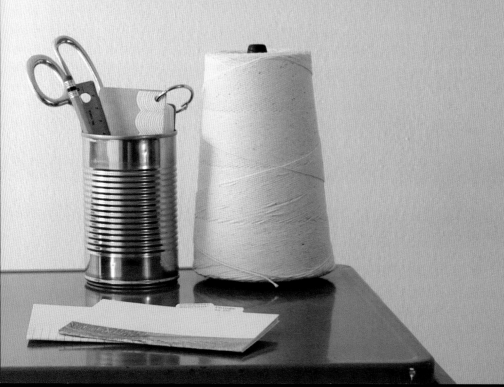

IDEA FILE

Index card dividers serve as covers for each one of these little flutter books. Create a set of books, and use them to keep track of books to read, computer passwords, ideas, memories, places to go, favorite quotes, and more. Store them together in a 3" × 5" index card file box or recipe box.

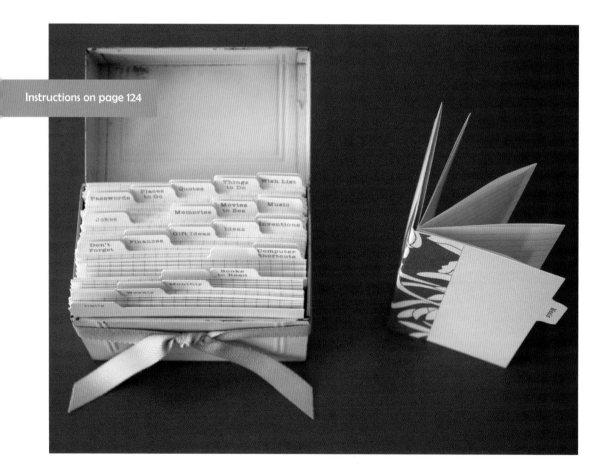

Instructions on page 124

SKETCH, JOT, JOURNAL

The cover of this book wraps around and tucks closed, much like a vintage postcard booklet. Fill the pages with drawings, writings, and anything else you would like to put on paper.

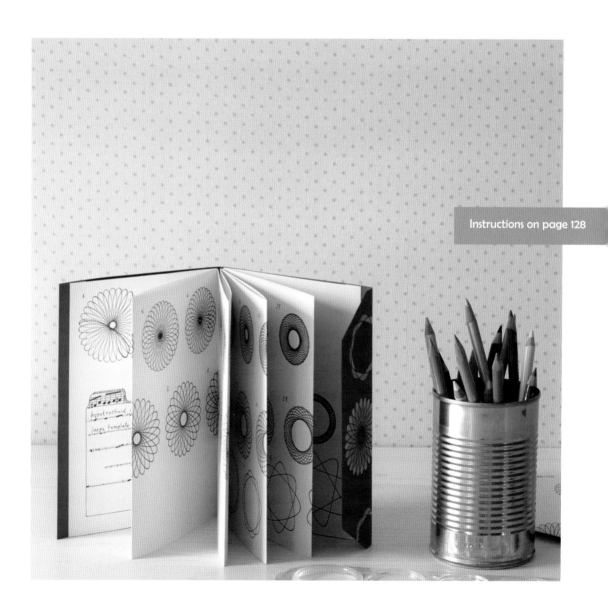

Instructions on page 128

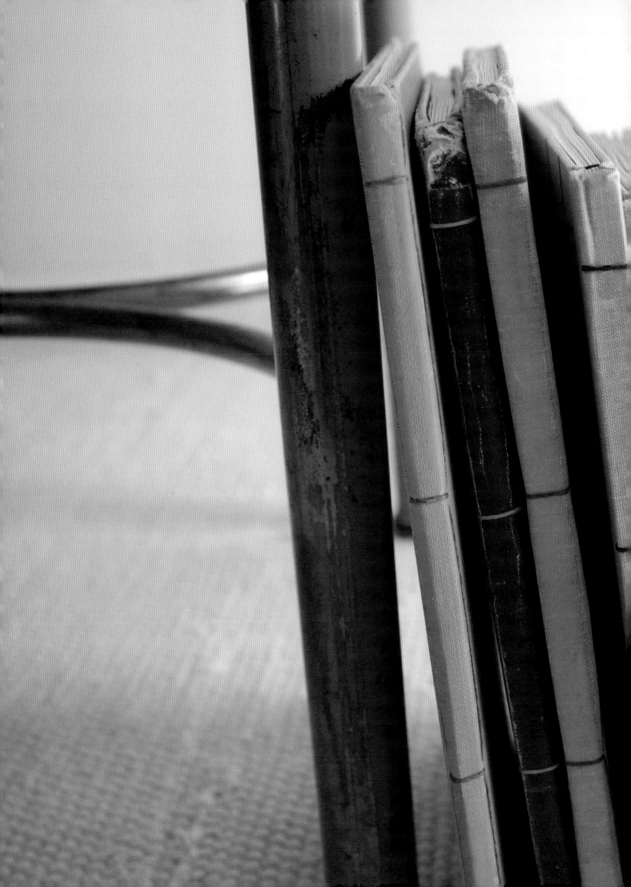

FOUR-HOLE BINDING AND VARIATIONS

Four-hole binding is what most people think of when they hear "Japanese bookbinding." Traditionally, these books are comprised of pages folded in half, with the folded edges at the fore edge of the book. The front and back covers are stitched to the pages through holes that penetrate all the way through the book, which is why these bindings are also often called stab bindings.

The four-hole binding forms the basis of three main variations: the noble, hemp-leaf, and tortoise-shell bindings. You don't have to stop there, though. Try using the basic pattern and adding your own variations. You can adapt the pattern to all sizes of books and to a variety of materials.

Although traditional stab bindings are held together with a special inner binding within the covers, the projects in this book are adapted for use with western papers and materials. You can use a bulldog clip in place of an inner binding while you stitch, and in special circumstances, you can apply paste to strengthen the spine.

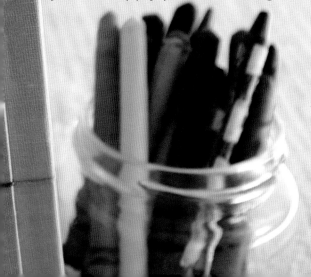

TAG NOTEBOOK

Two tags of the same size serve as the covers for this notebook. You can use inventory tags, luggage tags, or blank manila tags that you decorate yourself. The strings from each tag tie together to keep the book closed.

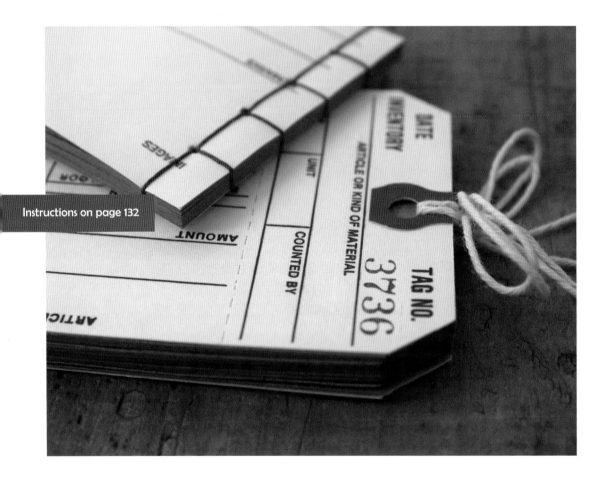

Instructions on page 132

RETURN-TO-SENDER MAIL BOOK

Fill up the pages of this book, seal the end closed, and send it through the mail to someone special. They can then add to the pages, reseal it, and send it back to you.

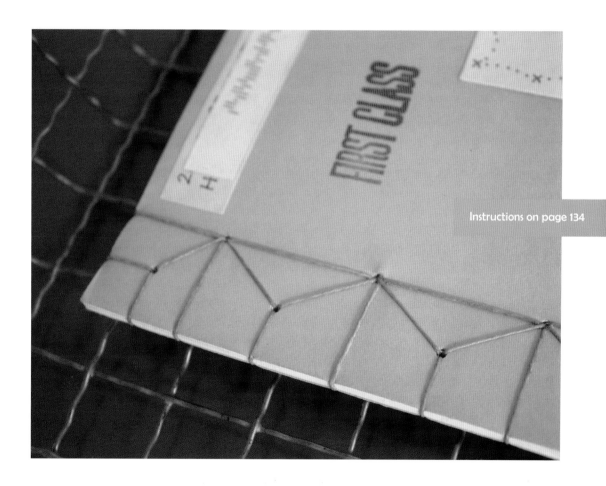

Instructions on page 134

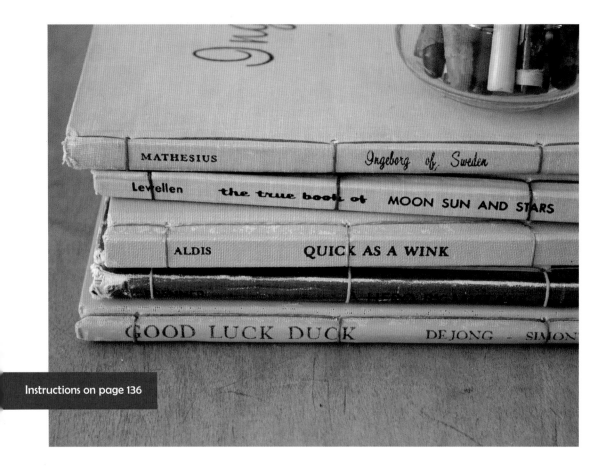

Instructions on page 136

RECYCLE BIN BOOK

Transform an old book, destined for the recycle bin, into a brand-new journal. The cover of a vintage children's book is filled with blank pages and rebound on the outside of the cover with a traditional Japanese four-hole binding. Now is your chance to rewrite the books!

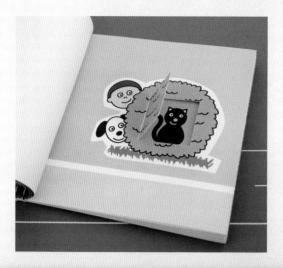

PEEK-A-BOOK

The pages of this book include small doors that reveal pictures cut from magazines and other printed sources. Create this book with a child in mind, and include their favorite things on each page.

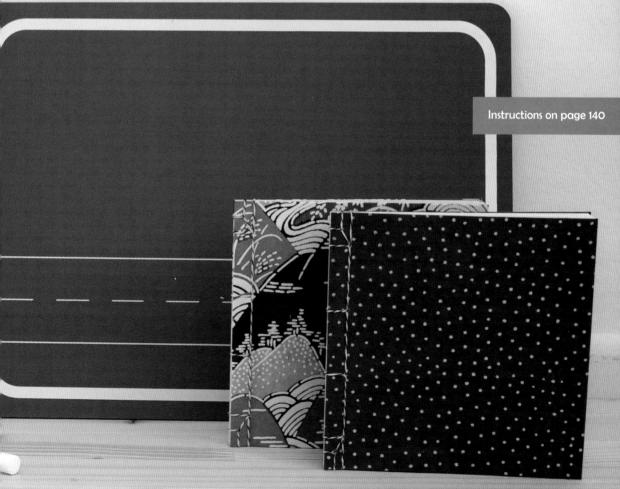

Instructions on page 140

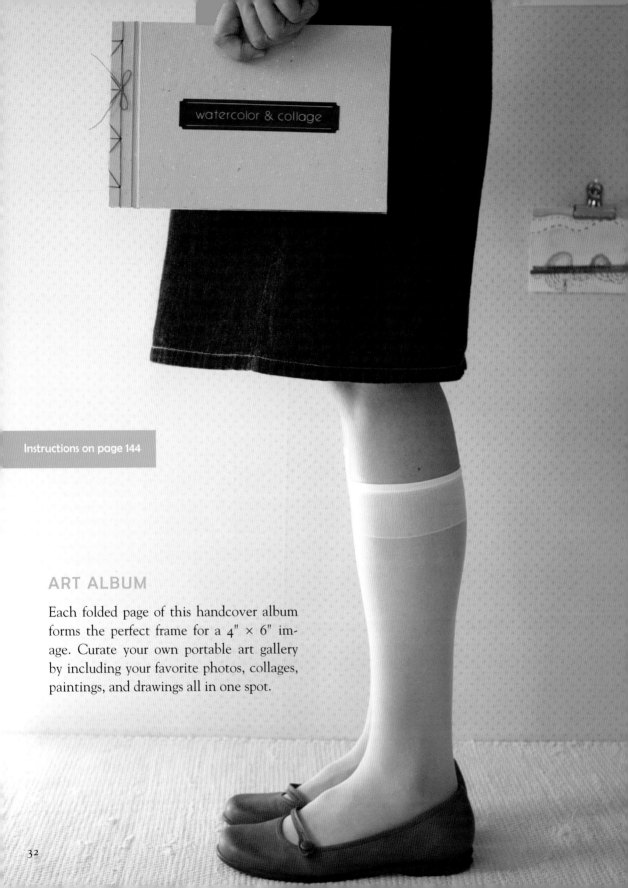

watercolor & collage

Instructions on page 144

ART ALBUM

Each folded page of this handcover album forms the perfect frame for a 4" × 6" image. Curate your own portable art gallery by including your favorite photos, collages, paintings, and drawings all in one spot.

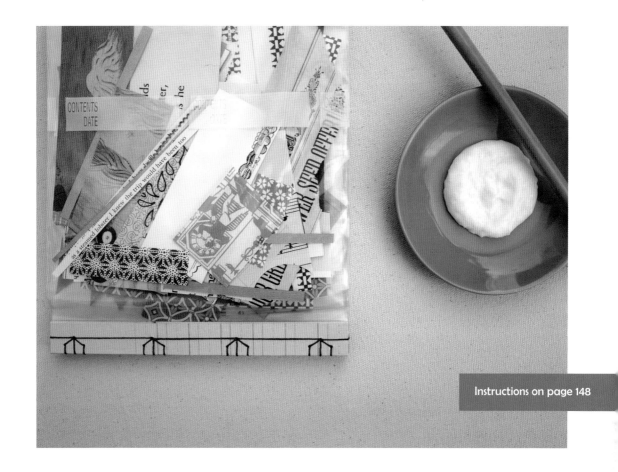

Instructions on page 148

CUT, KEEP, COLLAGE STORAGE BOOK

Plastic zipper bags form the pages of this unique book. Use it to store small papers and ephemera for collage projects. You may even find inspiration in the colors and patterns visible through the transparent pages.

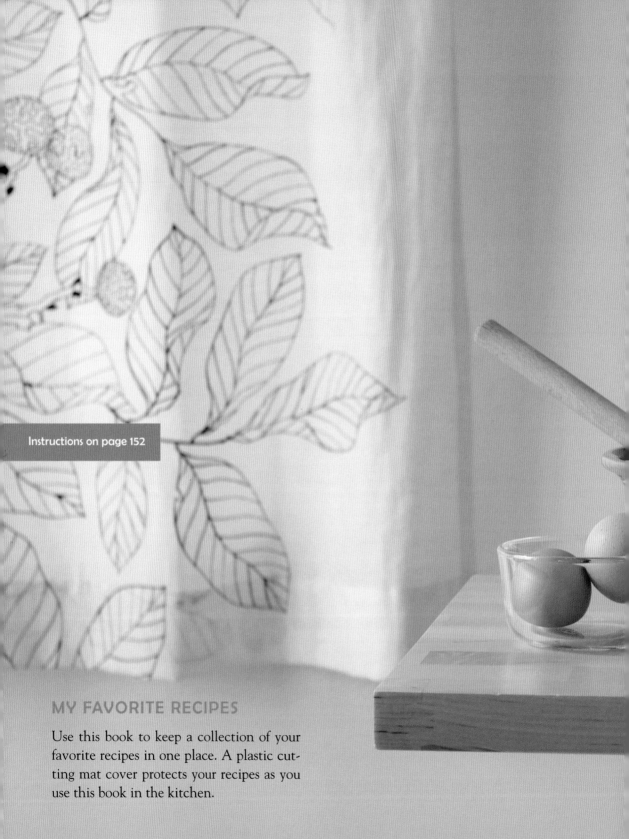

Instructions on page 152

MY FAVORITE RECIPES

Use this book to keep a collection of your favorite recipes in one place. A plastic cutting mat cover protects your recipes as you use this book in the kitchen.

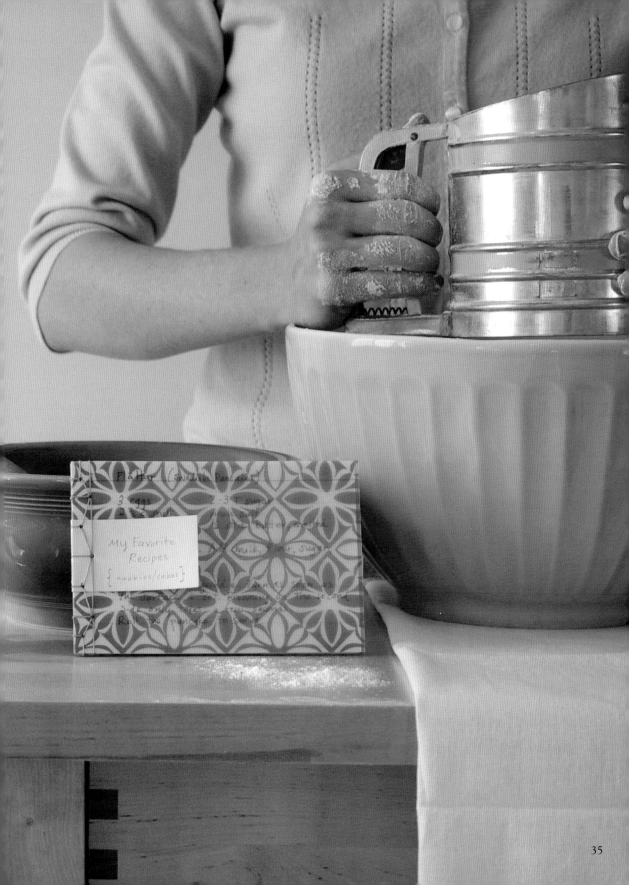

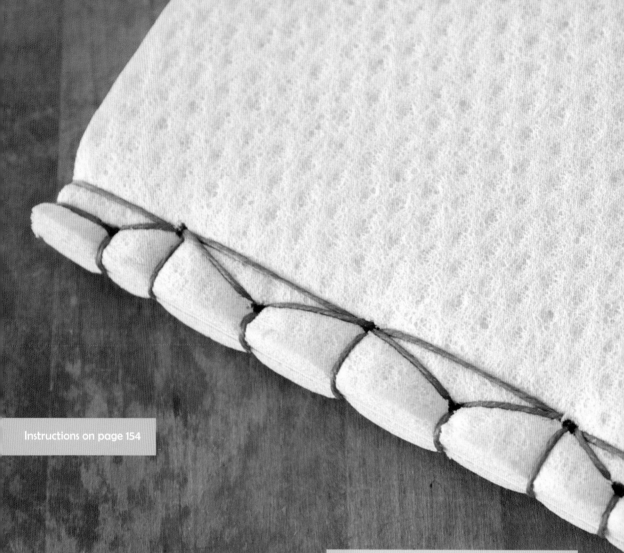

Instructions on page 154

MY FAVORITE CLEANING RECIPES

As a variation of My Favorite Recipes, a sponge serves as this book's cover instead of a plastic cutting mat. Use it to store a collection of cleaning recipes made from kitchen ingredients.

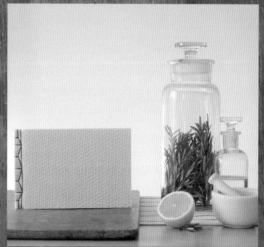

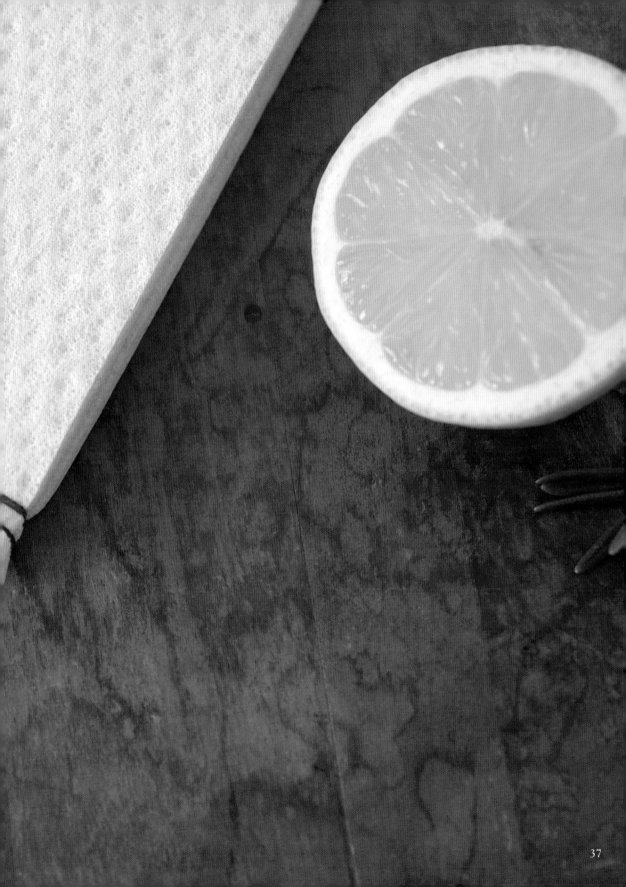

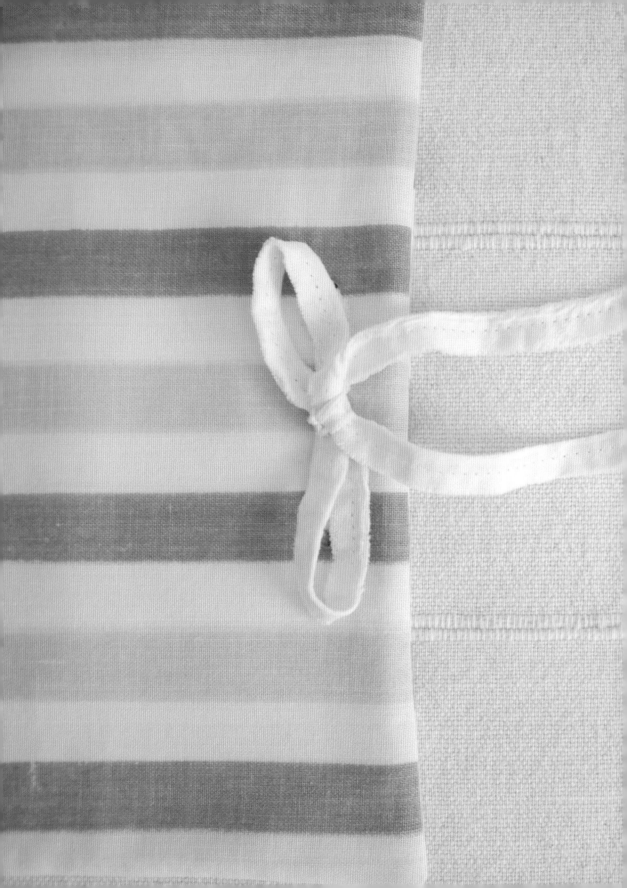

YAMATO BINDING

Also a stab binding, the Yamato binding is a simple book made by stitching through two holes. The ribbon or string used to bind your projects ties to the outside of the front cover.

P.S. LETTER COLLECTION

This project gathers correspondence from someone special into one place. Letters, cards, postcards, and envelopes are layered together and carefully bound with a simple Yamato binding.

Instructions on page 156

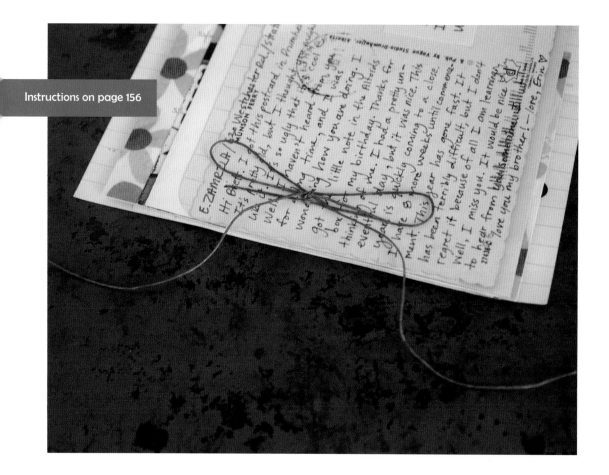

LEAFLET MEMO PAD

A leaf tracing makes a great pattern for this simple little memo pad that is inspired by nature. Create a collection of books, each made in a different leaf shape.

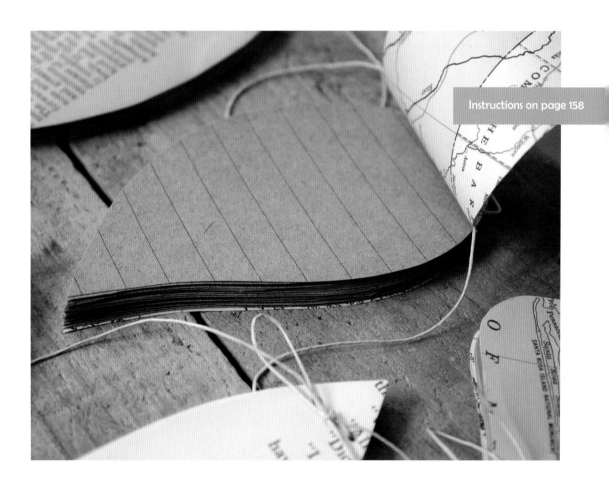

Instructions on page 158

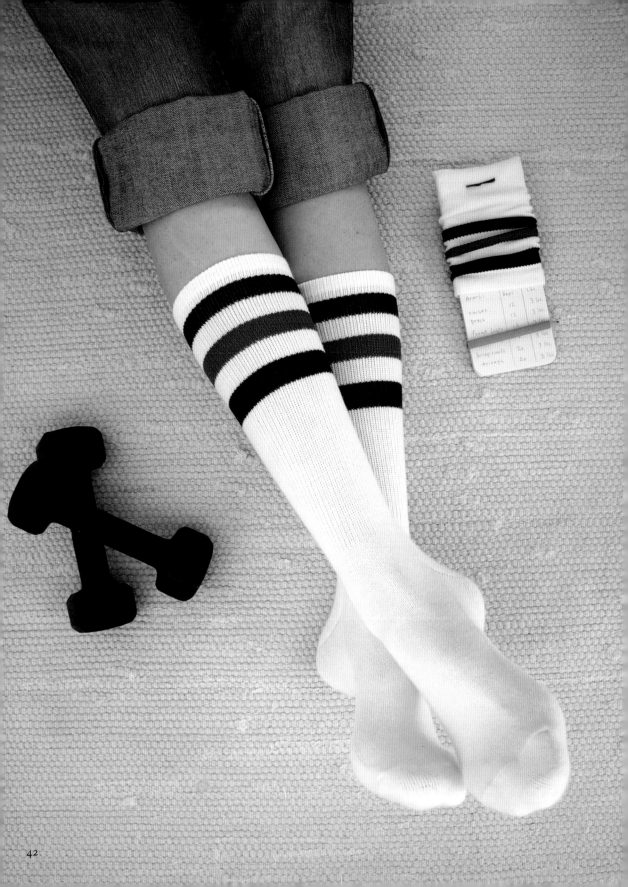

SOCK BOOK

A stretchy and soft sock makes an unusual, but functional book cover. Toss this sock book into your gym bag to keep notes on the go. Just scrunch back the sock to reveal the paper pages inside.

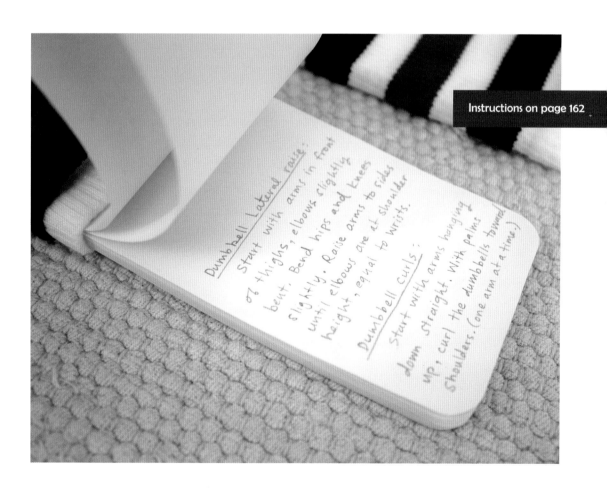

Instructions on page 162

PILLOWCASE DREAM JOURNAL

You may become sleepy as you jot down your dreams in this book. A variation of the Sock Book, the cover of this book is sewn from a vintage pillowcase. It is a bit more challenging to create, but worth the effort.

Instructions on page 166

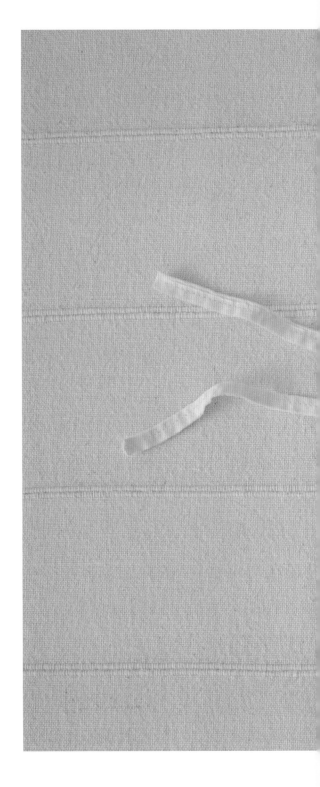

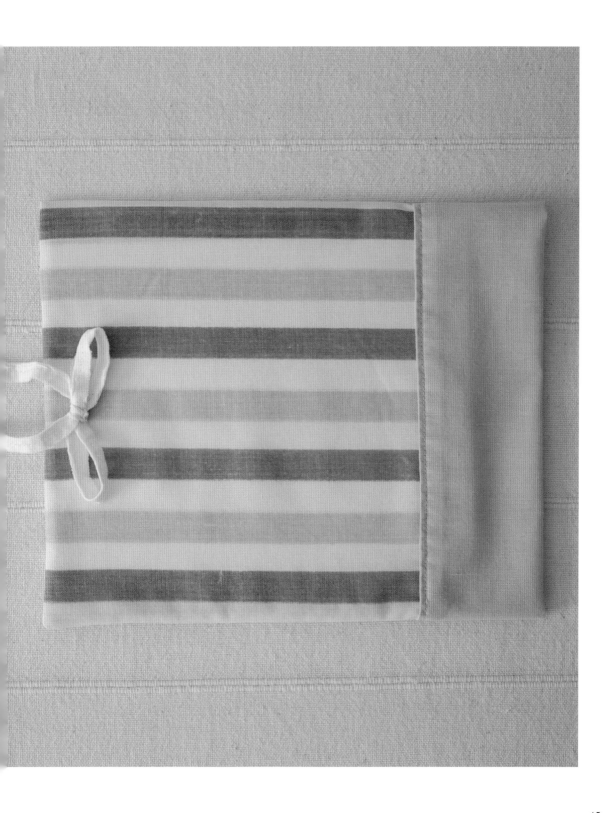

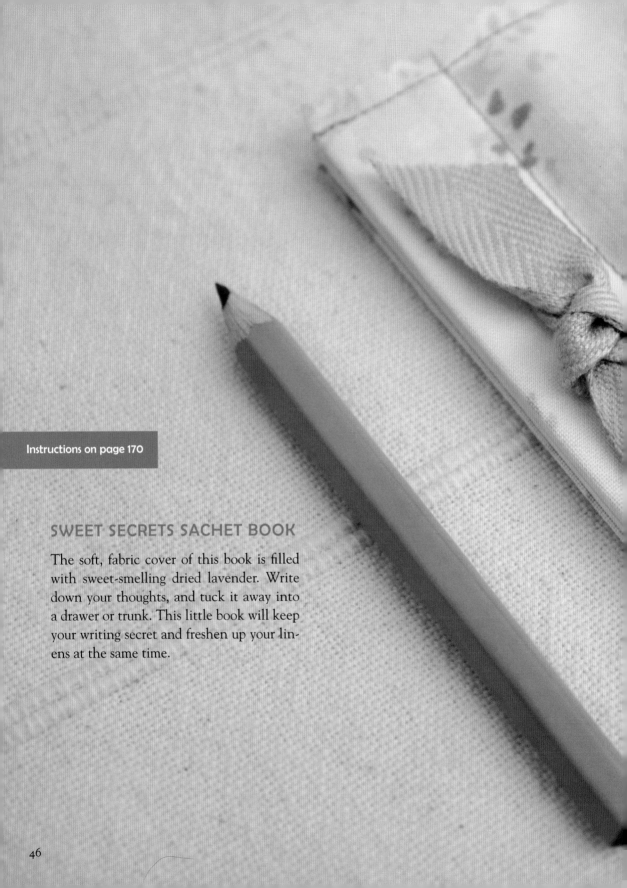

Instructions on page 170

SWEET SECRETS SACHET BOOK

The soft, fabric cover of this book is filled with sweet-smelling dried lavender. Write down your thoughts, and tuck it away into a drawer or trunk. This little book will keep your writing secret and freshen up your linens at the same time.

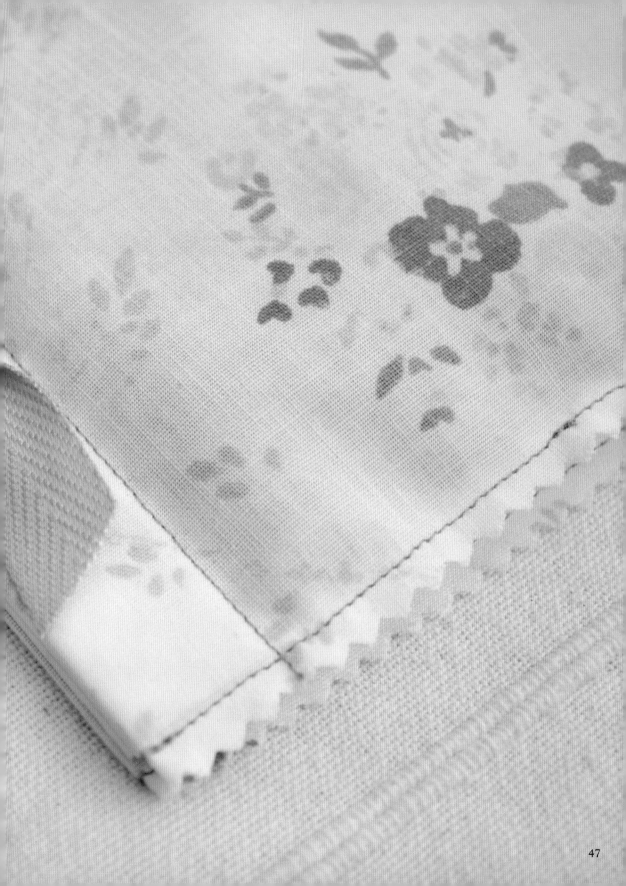

SEWING NOTIONS PINCUSHION BOOK

This variation of the Sweet Secrets Sachet Book is filled with polyester stuffing instead of lavender and serves as a pincushion. Store your sewing tips and notes on the inside and your pins and needles on the outside.

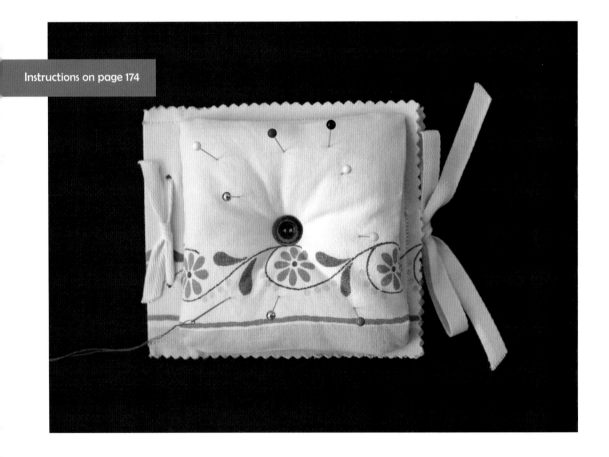

Instructions on page 174

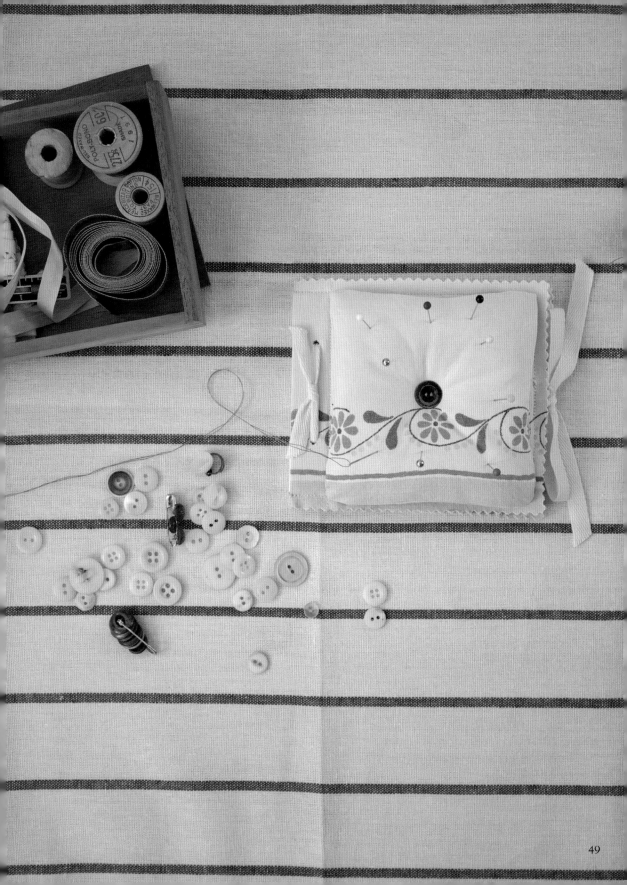

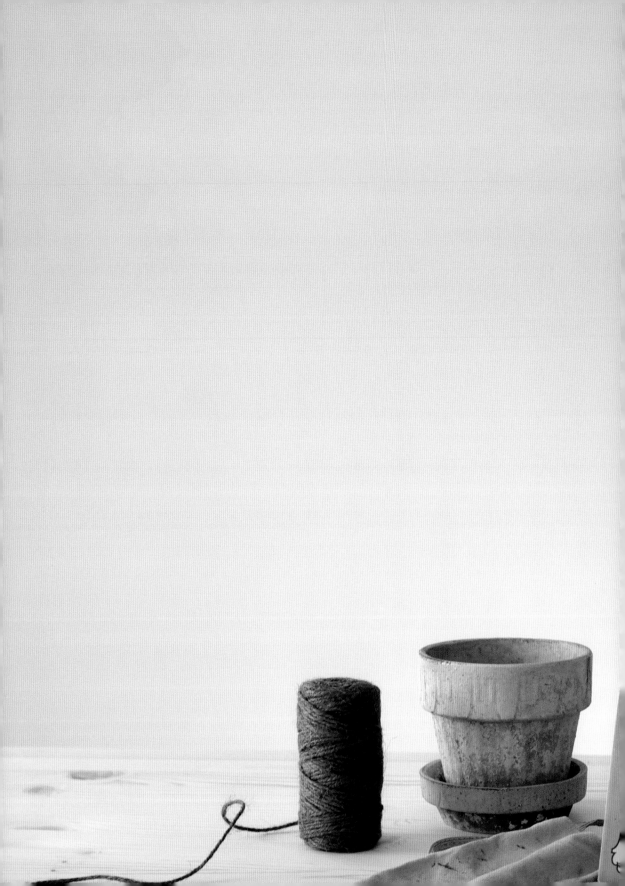

ACCOUNT BOOKS

This book is a type of ledger, which was traditionally used as a merchant's account book. The long strings that extend off the binding served the purpose of preservation: if a fire broke out, the books could be tossed into a well, hanging by the strings until they were later fetched. Nowadays, you can use the strings to hang your books wherever you like.

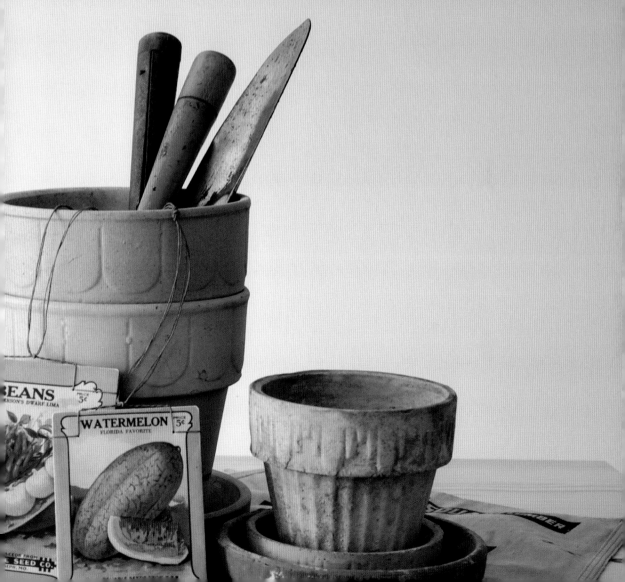

TEA BAG TRACING BOOK

The pages of this book are created from tea bags. If you are an avid tea drinker, you will collect the pages in no time. The transparent quality of the pages makes a perfect tracing book. You can trace the pictures in the morning newspaper as you sit and sip your tea!

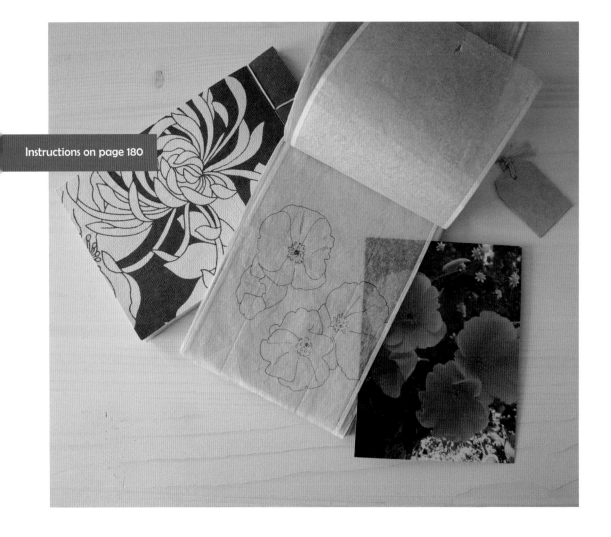

Instructions on page 180

GARDENER'S JOURNAL

Once you plant your seeds, jot down notes on how to care for them in this little journal. The covers are made from seed packets and the account book binding provides a string for hanging this journal next to your gardening tools.

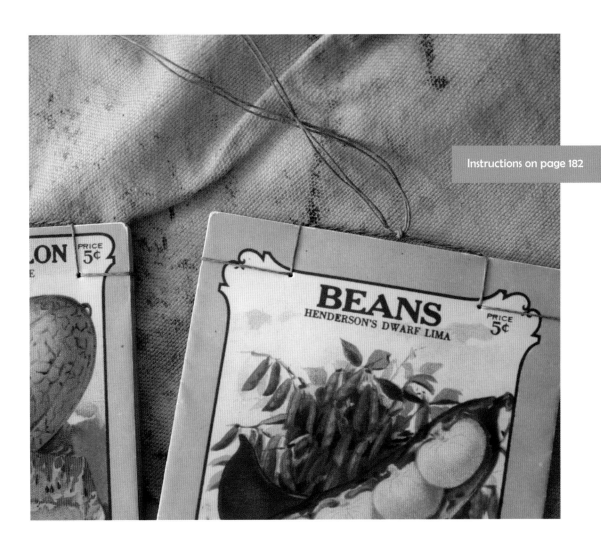

Instructions on page 182

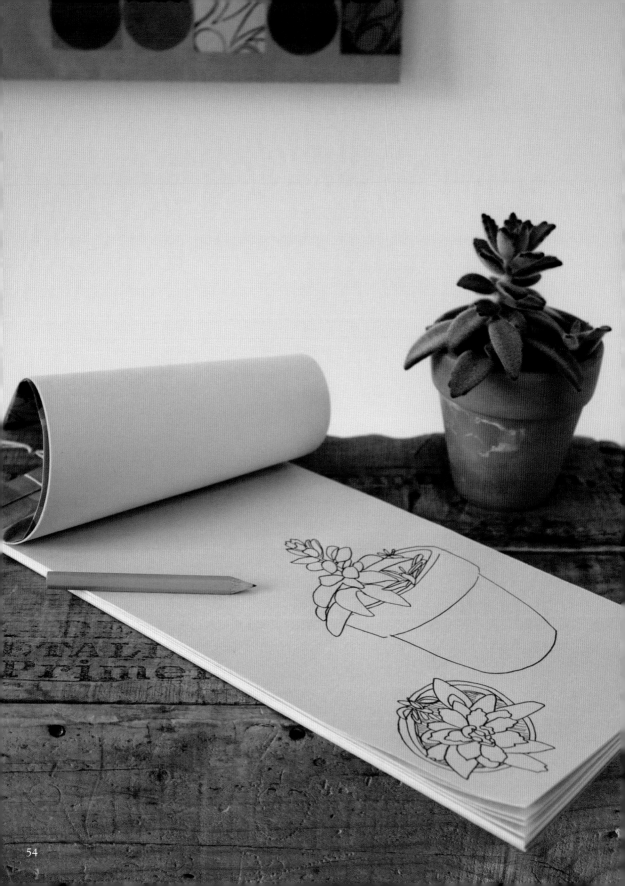

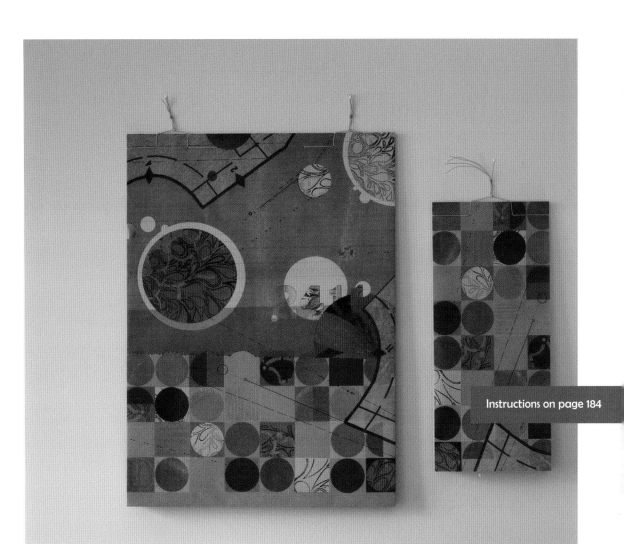

Instructions on page 184

WALL ART DRAWING PAD

Reuse a favorite calendar image or poster as the cover for this drawing pad. Filled with drawing paper, this book can hang on your wall to serve as a functional work of art.

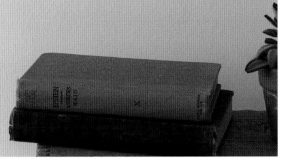

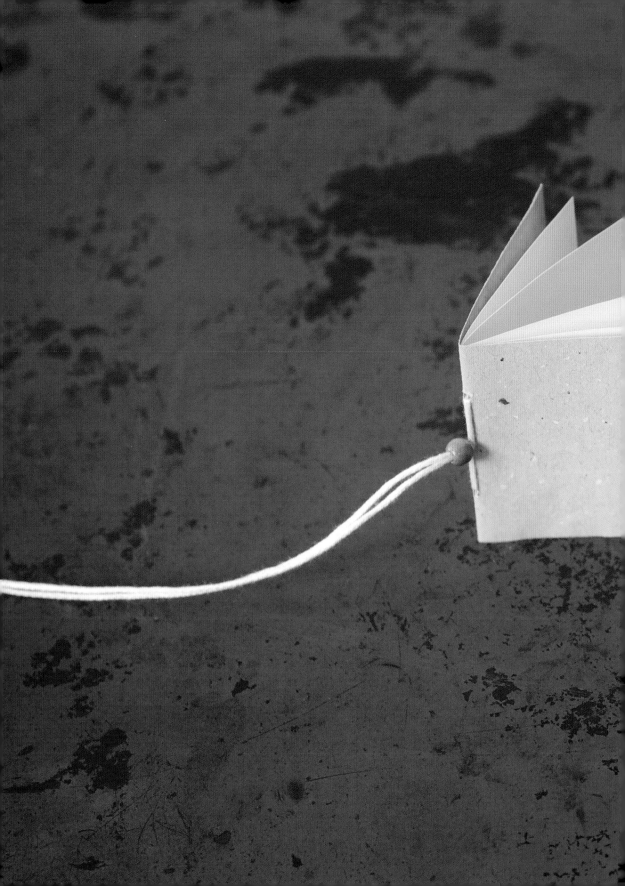

Ledger books are quick and easy to make. Pages are folded in half and sewn together along the fold. The small size and number of pages makes this a great project for using up leftover paper scraps from other projects.

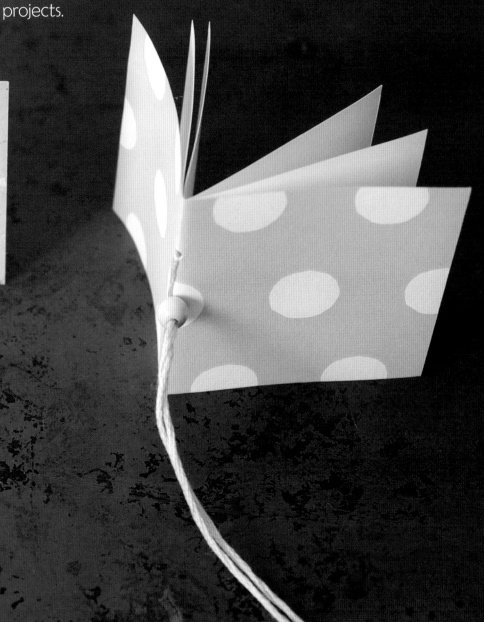

GIFT TAG BOOK

This little book is created from gift wrap. The binding is simple and includes a long string for tying it to a package. Use this book to send a note of good cheer to the lucky recipient.

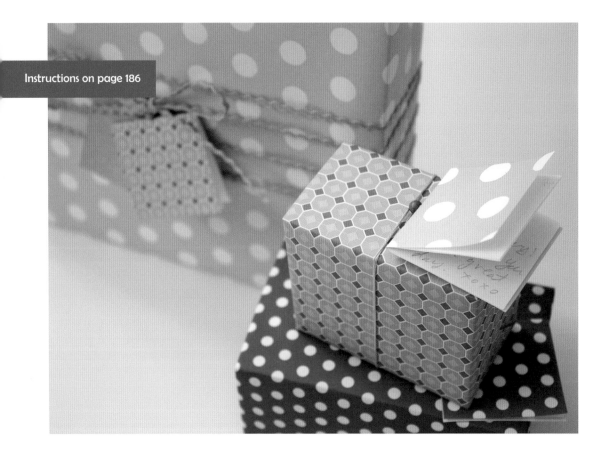

Instructions on page 186

RECYCLE BIN MEMO PAD

After making a book or two, you will surely have paper scraps to spare! Turn your leftover scraps into a memo pad with this project. Use it to keep lists and notes.

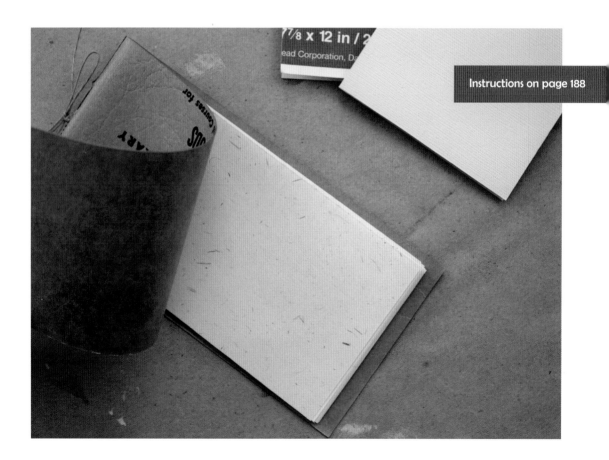

Instructions on page 188

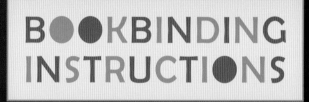

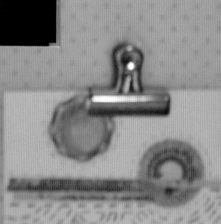

BOOKBINDING TOOLS AND MATERIALS

Many bookbinding tools and materials are used for a variety of other arts and crafts. This makes collecting them fairly easy. You may discover that you already have many of these supplies.

The basic ingredients for a book include paper and string. Tools for cutting, pasting, punching, and stitching turn these basic ingredients into a finished product.

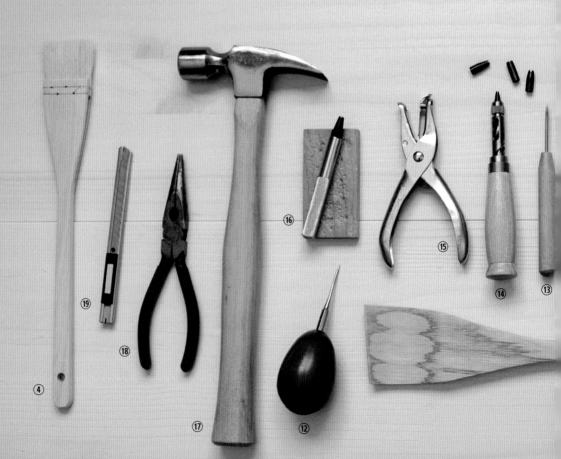

Tools

Several tool options are shown, but you do not need to collect them all. The most important tools in the list below are starred. Most of these tools are available at arts and crafts supply stores.

1. **Large all-purpose craft brush:** The bristles on this inexpensive brush are trimmed down to 1", making them stiff. This brush is ideal for applying paste to larger surface areas and useful for smoothing.
2. ***Small all-purpose craft brush:** These brushes come in a variety of sizes. This one is also trimmed down to 1". Use a smaller brush when working with smaller surface areas.
3. **Paintbrush:** Use this brush to apply paste to small areas.
4. **Japanese Hake brush:** This soft-bristled brush is traditionally used for watercolor and calligraphy and comes in a variety of sizes. You can also use it to apply paste.
5. **Calligraphy brush:** Use this brush to apply paste to small areas.
6. **Wood potter's rib:** This inexpensive tool is great for smoothing and burnishing paper.
7. **Clay modeling tool:** Use the smooth end for burnishing paper folds.
8. **Wood spatula:** This ubiquitous kitchen tool works well for smoothing and burnishing paper.
9. ***Bone folder:** One of the most versatile bookbinding tools, a bone folder is made to score, smooth, and burnish paper. Sharpen with sandpaper as needed.
10. **Beeswax:** Apply wax to your thread for smoother stitching through paper. Waxed thread is especially useful for stab bindings.
11. ***Binder's needle and tapestry needle:** Look for a needle with an eye large enough to accommodate your thread. A blunt tip helps to save your fingers while stitching.
12. **Heavy-duty awl:** The rounded wood handle of this awl protects your hand, and the steel tip can punch through thick stacks of paper. Always use it on a protective surface.
13. ***Paper awl:** This tool also punches through thick stacks of paper. Always use it on a protective surface.
14. **Japanese screw punch and bits:** A screw punch twists as you push it down to cut smoothly through paper and fabric. You can punch through several pieces of paper at a time but not through thick stacks of paper or book board. Interchangeable bits come in a variety of sizes. Always use it on a protective surface.
15. **Single-hole hand punch:** You will find this tool among office supplies. The standard hole size is ¼"; smaller hole sizes are also available.
16. **Hollow punch and protective surface:** Use a heavy-duty hollow punch to create holes in book board and stacks of paper. Tap the tool with a hammer, and always use it on a protective surface. These punches often come in a variety of sizes.
17. **Small hammer:** This tool is used with a hollow punch.

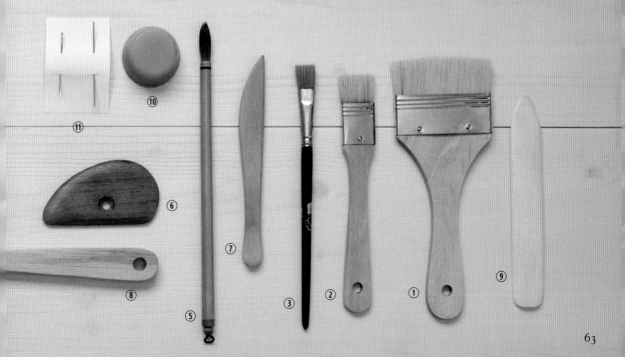

18. **Needle-nose pliers:** A basic pair will assist you in pulling your needle and thread through thick stacks of paper. You can also use these pliers to work with wire.

19. ***Craft or utility knife:** Use a small craft knife to trim papers. Use a larger utility knife to cut through book board and other thick materials. Always keep a sharp blade, and use this tool on a protective surface.

20. **Book press:** This tool provides pressure to flatten and smooth projects as they dry. You can easily substitute a heavy stack of books or a few bricks to press your projects instead.

*Metal ruler: Use this tool to measure and also as a guide for cutting straight lines with a craft knife. A cork backing is recommended to prevent slipping.

*Self-healing cutting mat: A surface to protect your table while cutting and punching holes is important. Cutting mats are available in a variety of sizes.

*Bulldog clip: Look through your office supplies to find one of these handy clips. Use it to hold pages together while punching holes and binding.

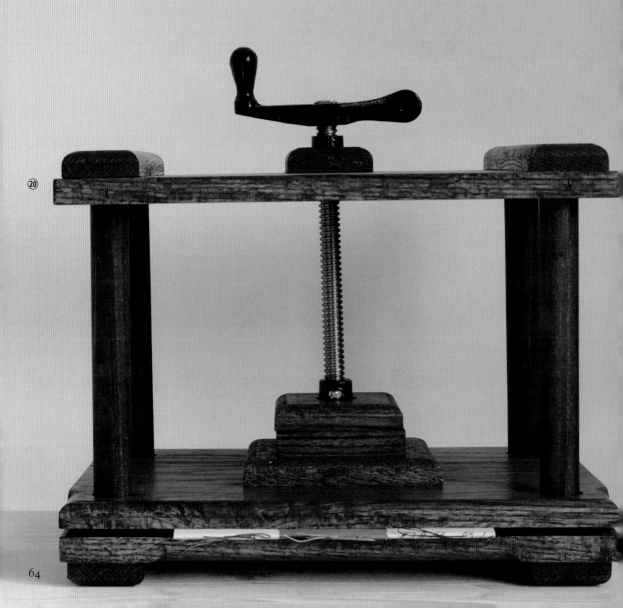

Thread, Ribbon, Cord, and String

The best binding materials are very strong and do not stretch. Waxed linen thread is a favorite of bookbinders, but many other options are available. Traditional Japanese books are bound with silk thread. Keep an eye out for interesting cord and string in the jewelry and sewing sections of your craft store.

1. Hemp cord
2. Ribbon
3. Twill tape
4. Rickrack

5. Baby rickrack
6. Baker's twine
7. Waxed linen thread
8. Embroidery floss

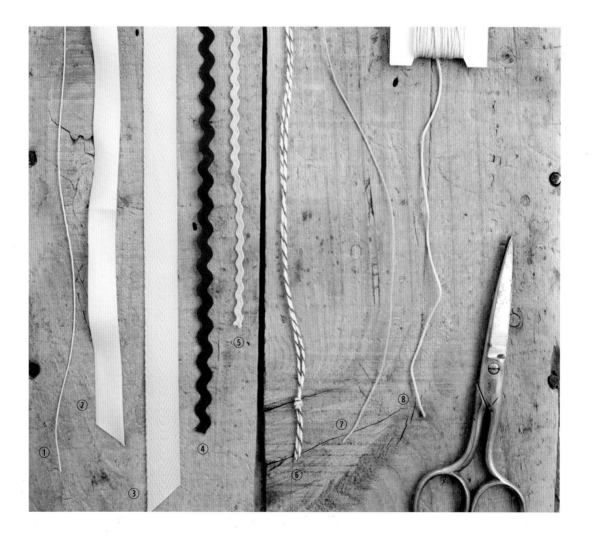

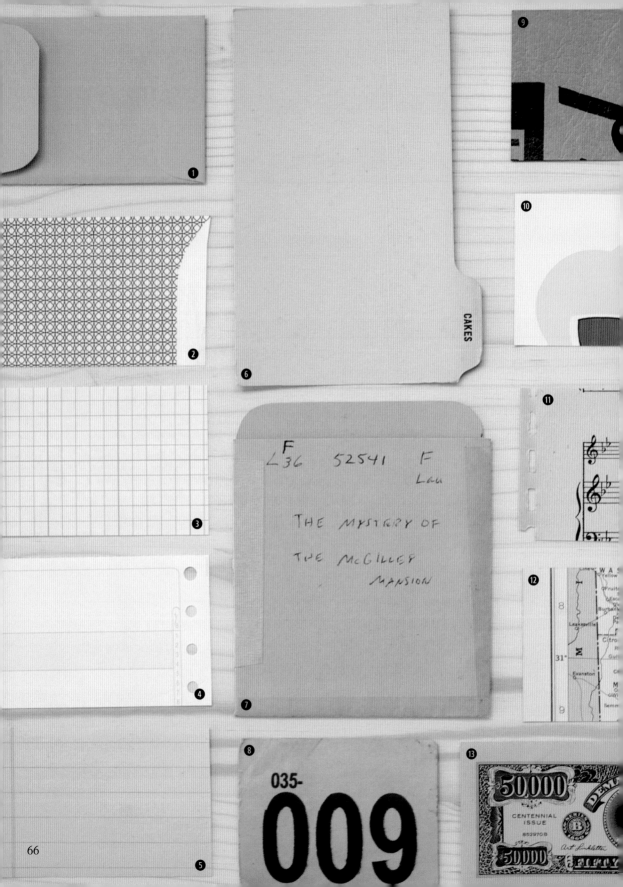

CAKES

F
L36   52541   F
                  Lau

THE MYSTERY OF

THE McGILLEY

        MANSION

035-
009

50000
CENTENNIAL
ISSUE
85297GB
50000   FIFTY

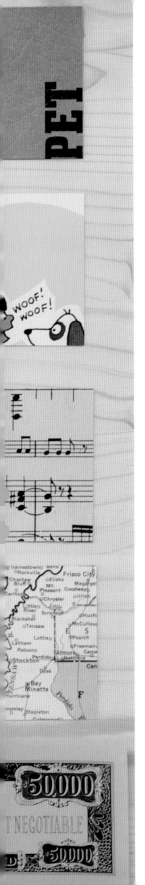

Papers

Paper is available in all thicknesses, textures, and colors. Traditional Japanese bookbinding utilizes Japanese papers, which have a wonderful texture, strength, and flexibility to them. Western papers are a bit different from Japanese papers, but they can be used in many of the same ways. Remember to consider the direction of the grain when choosing papers for specific projects.

For the inside pages of your projects, you will use text weight paper, which is about the thickness of printer paper. For pages that will hold photos, try paper that is just a bit thicker than text weight paper, such as heavy weight drawing paper. Card stock is thicker yet and works well for small book covers. For hard book covers, begin with a core of bookbinder's board, or Davey board, and cover it with decorative paper.

Take the opportunity to be creative with your paper selections. Keep an eye out for interesting papers among things that you might normally throw away or recycle, such as food packaging and junk mail. Any of these examples of papers can be used for your book projects:

1. Coin envelope
2. Security envelope pattern
3. Grid paper
4. Green bar computer paper
5. Ruled paper
6. Index or recipe divider
7. Library pocket
8. Ticket stub
9. Card stock from notebook
10. Printed ephemera
11. Sheet music
12. Map
13. Play money

14. Handmade paper
15. Drawings on plain paper
16. Decorative Japanese paper
17. Wrapping paper
18. Origami
19. Paper stencil
20. Playing card
21. Handwriting an old recipe card
22. Manila tag

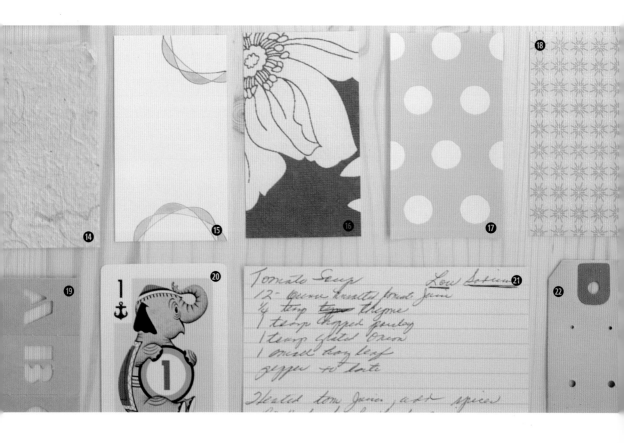

Adhesives

Although three variations of cooked wheat paste are the primary adhesives of traditional Japanese bookbinding, you are welcome to use the adhesive with which you are most comfortable. Many options are available.

Wheat starch paste: This archival adhesive is sold in powder form. To use, add water and cook the mixture to the desired consistency (it should come with instructions). One of the benefits of using paste is that the adhesion is reversible: only water is needed to remove and repair the pasted portions. Wheat starch paste can be adjusted to any consistency, from watery to thick. The main drawback is that the wet paste can grow mold if you keep it around too long. Place it in the refrigerator to make it last longer. I often mix wheat starch paste with PVA for a smoother consistency. PVA is not reversible, so if you mix it, the paste will lose its archival quality.

PVA: Another name for white glue, this adhesive dries acid free and is found almost anywhere. If it is too thick, add water to thin it, or mix it with prepared wheat starch paste. PVA creates a permanent bond.

Glue stick: A permanent, acid-free glue stick will often do the trick. Use it to paste small areas together. I do not recommend using a glue stick when covering book board or gluing large surfaces together.

Double-sided tape: Look for an artists' quality tape. You may be able to find an acid-free tape, but it is rare, so do not use this on important projects.

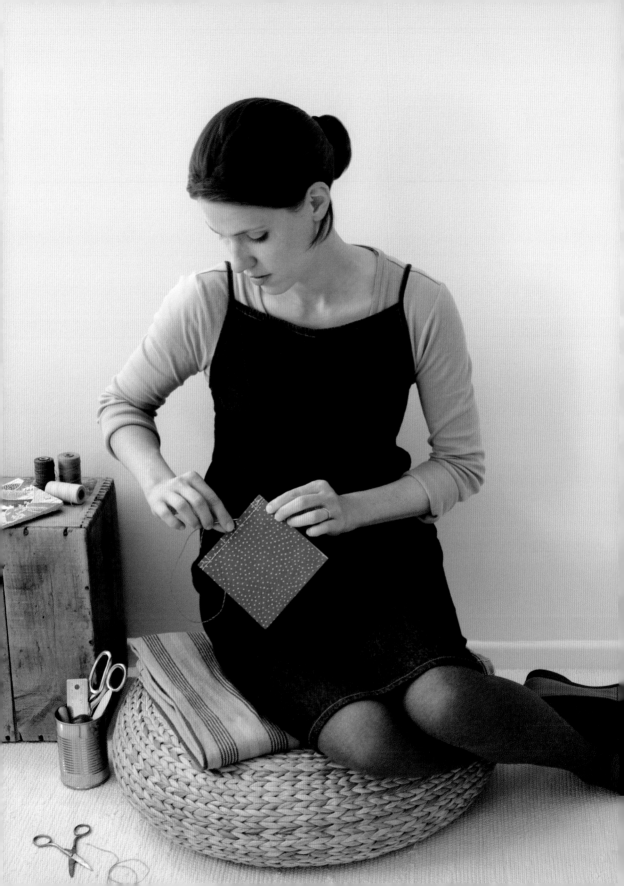

BOOKBINDING BASICS

Before beginning on the projects, you will need to learn just a few basics. You will notice several bookbinding terms used throughout the projects. These terms are explained in the Structure and Techniques sections. The stitches at the heart of Japanese bookbinding are included in the Stitching Techniques section (see page 74).

Structure

You will notice these terms used in many of the project instructions.

Book block: The stack of pages between the covers, sometimes referred to as "text."

Covers: Outer material that protects the inside pages. The front cover and the back cover sandwich the pages between them.

Endpaper: A decorative paper pasted to the inside of the front or back cover.

Fore edge: The right edge of a book, opposite of the spine.

Head: The top edge of a book.

Hinge: A flexible fold in a cover that allows the cover to easily open and close.

Paper grain: The direction in which the fibers lie. It is important that the grain of the paper runs parallel to the spine. This allows the cover and pages to open easily. (See the Techniques section for ways to determine the direction of the paper grain.)

Spine: The left edge of a book, where the book is bound.

Tail: The bottom edge of a book, opposite of the head.

Text: The stack of pages between the covers, sometimes referred to as a "book block."

Title strip: A rectangular strip of paper pasted to the front cover, displaying the book's title.

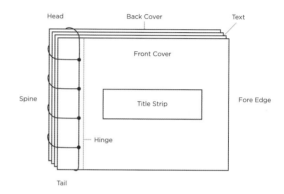

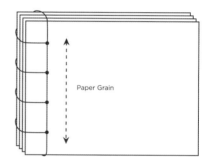

Techniques

Most bookbinding techniques are fairly simple, but do be careful, especially when using sharp knives and awls. Always cut away from yourself; when you are stitching, pull your needle away from yourself. Keep a clean workspace, and protect your tabletop with a cutting mat when using sharp tools and waxed paper when using adhesives.

Burnish: To smooth a fold. Lay your paper on a flat surface and slide the long, flat side of a bone folder or wood tool along a folded edge.

Cut: To trim materials to desired size. You can use either scissors or a craft knife and metal ruler to cut your papers. When using a craft, or utility, knife, always cut on a protective surface. Use extra caution when cutting through book board and other thick materials. You will need to use a fresh blade and make several passes in order to cut all the way through.

Fold: To create a crease by bending one part of a paper over another part of itself. Whenever possible fold paper along the grain of the paper. This is particularly important with accordion books where the grain of the paper should run parallel to the fold.

You can use a couple ways to discover the grain of your paper. If you tear a strip of paper along the grain, it will tear in a smooth, straight line. If you tear a strip of paper against the grain, it will tear in a jagged, irregular line. Another way to find the paper grain is to lay a sheet of paper flat on a table. Gently lift the right side over toward the left side (do not completely fold) and notice how flat the page lies. Try this again, bringing the top side over toward the bottom side. The page will be more flexible as you fold along with the grain. The page will be more resistant to folding against the grain.

Nest: To place one page into the fold of another. When working with projects that are folded along the spine, you will often nest the inside pages into the cover, placing the folded edge of the pages against the inside fold of the cover.

Paste or glue: To adhere papers. Always start with a fresh layer of waxed paper to protect your work surface. If you are using wet paste or glue to adhere papers together, apply a thin layer to one paper with a paste brush.

Carefully lay the pasted page in place. In most cases, you will smooth and press your papers after pasting. It is important to rinse your paste brush well, just after you use it.

Press: To apply pressure to a project. You can use either a book press or a heavy stack of books or bricks. Most often, you will press freshly pasted materials so they dry completely flat. Sandwich your projects in clean waxed paper before pressing and allow them to completely dry before removing.

Punch: To create a hole in your paper. Several punching tools provide different hole sizes. Make a hole that accommodates the size of your thread or ribbon.

Score: To create a crease with a bone folder or other tool prior to folding. The best technique is to place a metal ruler on top of your paper where you want to create a score line. Slide the pointed end of a bone folder along the ruler, pressing down into the paper. Scoring does not cut through; it allows covers and pages to open more easily.

Smooth: To gently remove bubbles and wrinkles from freshly pasted papers. Use either a brush or the long, flat side of a bone folder or wood tool. Carefully smooth from the top side, moving your tool from the center toward the edges.

Thread a needle: To prepare a needle and thread for stitching. When stitching bookbinding projects, you will use a single thread. Take one end of the thread through the eye of a needle and pull about 4" of thread through. The longer portion of the thread is what you will use to bind your book.

Tie off: To tie the remaining threads together after binding to prevent the stitching from unraveling.

Double knot: To tie an overhand knot in the same place, twice in a row.

STITCHING TECHNIQUES

Most of the Japanese bindings are stab bindings. The covers are stitched to the pages through holes that penetrate all the way through the book from front to back. The exception is the ledger binding, which is sewn along the fold.

The pages of traditional stab bindings are held together with a special inner binding within the covers. The projects in this book are adapted for use with a basic bulldog clip instead of an inner binding. Use a clip at the fore edge of your book block to hold the pages together while you stitch. You may even use a clip on the outside of the cover if the materials that you are working with allow it. Always place a thick piece of paper underneath the clip to protect your cover and pages from damage.

Each binding has its own traditional measurements, which are presented with the instructions for each stitch, for placement of the holes. From text weight or scrap paper, create a template paper the same size as the pages or cover of your book. Mark the holes on this template with a pencil and ruler, and use it as a guide to punch holes in the covers and pages. The measurements provided for each binding are just guidelines. Once you get the hang of the bindings use the same ratios provided to make larger books. Experiment by adding more holes or placing them at different distances from the spine and from each other.

The amount of thread you will need varies for each project. The thickness of your pages, the distance of the holes from the spine, and the number of holes all affect the thread length. You will often use more thread than you think! It is better to start with too much and trim the excess at the end. If you run short while stitching, take your needle through a hole in the cover and into the pages to tie on another length of thread. Leave the knot concealed between the pages and continue stitching from there. (All of the projects in this book have a suggested thread length.)

Use a strong thread that does not stretch, and pull it tight as you stitch. The larger the holes are in the cover and pages, the easier it is to pull the needle and thread through. Sometimes the needle may become difficult to pull through, especially when passing through the same hole several times. If this is the case, use a pair of pliers to grasp the end of the needle and pull it through. Be very careful to protect yourself and others when stitching. Always pull the needle away from yourself and others.

Japanese Four-Hole Binding

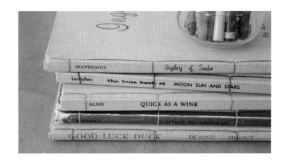

The Japanese four-hole binding is the most basic of the traditional Japanese stab bindings. It serves as the foundation for the other stab bindings.

1. This binding requires four holes. The standard alignment of the holes is ⅜" from the edge of the spine. Place the top hole ⅝" from the top edge of the book, place the bottom hole ⅝" from the bottom edge of the book, and place two more holes evenly between the first two holes. Mark the placement of each hole on a template paper cut to the same size as the top page or cover. You will use a length of thread five times the height of the spine.

2. You may leave a clip on the fore edge of your pages while you stitch, if you like. Place a small scrap of paper between the clip and your pages to prevent the clip from damaging your pages.

3. To begin, split apart your pages about halfway through the stack. Enter from the inside of the book through hole 2. Leave about 4" of thread inside the book. You will use this section of thread to tie off when you are finished stitching.

4. Place the pages back together in a stack and wrap your thread around the spine, entering hole 2 from back to front.

5. Proceed down the spine through hole 3 from front to back. Wrap the spine and enter hole 3 from front to back again. (Note: It may appear as though you are missing steps as you proceed down the spine. Don't worry; you will complete the missed areas as you work your way back up.)

6. Enter hole 4 from back to front. Wrap the spine and enter hole 4 from back to front again. Then wrap the bottom of the book and enter through hole 4 back to front a third time.

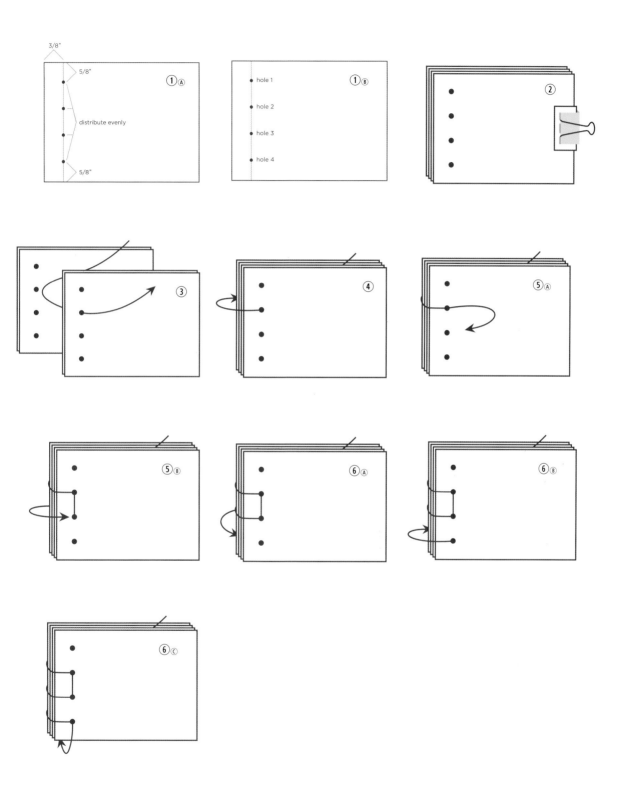

7. Proceed up the spine through hole 3 from front to back, through hole 2 from back to front, and then through hole 1 from front to back.

8. Wrap the spine and enter hole 1 from front to back. Then wrap the top of the book and enter hole 1 from front to back again.

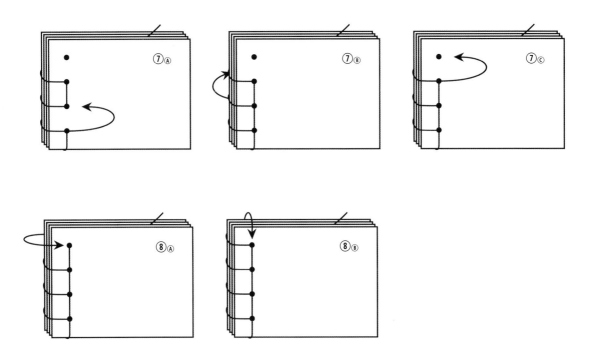

9. At this point, you are almost finished. Remove the clip, if you are using one. Carefully proceed through hole 2 from the back to the inside of the book where you began.

10. Open up your pages to the two threads. Tie the threads in a tight double knot, right up against hole 2 where they came through. Trim the threads to about ½" and carefully tuck them back into the stitched spine, hiding them from view.

11. The completed Japanese four-hole binding.

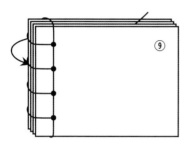

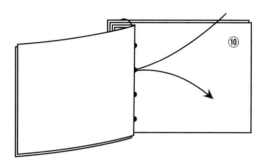

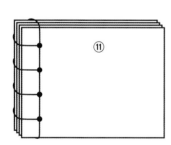

Noble Binding

The noble binding is the same as the Japanese four-hole binding, with a little extra twist.

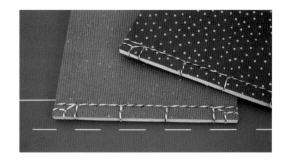

1. This binding requires six holes. The standard alignment of the four main holes is ⅜" from the edge of the spine. Place the top hole ⅝" from the top edge of the book, place the bottom hole ⅝" from the bottom edge of the book, and place two more holes evenly between the first two holes. Hole 1a and 4b align ³⁄₁₆" from the edge of the spine (halfway between the row of four holes and the spine). Place hole 1a ⁵⁄₁₆" from the top edge of the book and place hole 4b ⁵⁄₁₆" from the bottom edge of the book. Mark the placement of each hole on a template paper cut to the same size as the top page or cover. You will use a length of thread six times the height of the spine.

2. You may leave a clip on the fore edge of your pages while you stitch, if you like. Place a small scrap of paper between the clip and your pages to prevent the clip from damaging your pages.

3. To begin, split apart your pages about halfway through the stack. Enter from the inside of the book through hole 2. Leave about 4" of thread inside the book. You will use this section of thread to tie off when you are finished stitching.

4. Place the pages back together in a stack and wrap your thread around the spine, entering hole 2 from back to front.

5. Proceed down the spine through hole 3 from front to back. Wrap the spine and enter hole 3 from front to back again. (Note: It may appear as though you are missing steps as you proceed down the spine. Don't worry; you will complete the missed areas as you work your way back up.)

6. Enter hole 4 from back to front. Wrap the spine and enter hole 4 from back to front again. Then wrap the bottom of the book and enter through hole 4 a third time.

7. At this point, enter hole 4b from front to back. Wrap the spine and enter hole 4b front to back again.

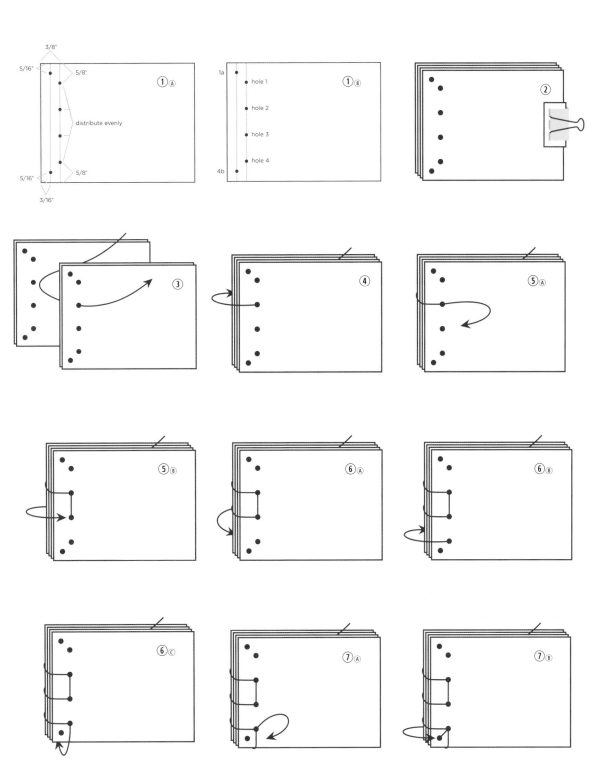

8. Wrap the bottom of the book and enter hole 4b front to back for a third time.

9. Complete the corner by entering hole 4 from back to front.

10. Proceed up the spine through hole 3 from front to back, through hole 2 from back to front, and then through hole 1 from front to back.

11. Wrap the spine and enter hole 1 from front to back again. Then wrap the top of the book and enter hole 1 from front to back a third time.

12. Enter hole 1a from back to front. Wrap the spine and enter hole 1a from back to front again.

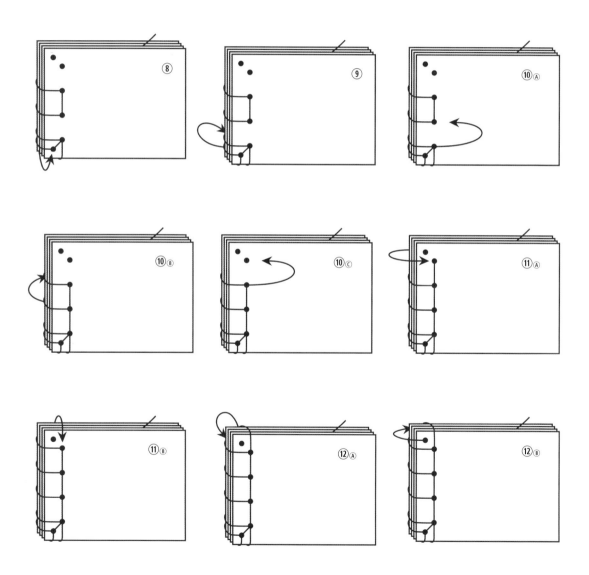

13. Wrap the top of the book and enter hole 1a back to front a third time.
14. Complete the top corner by entering hole 1 from front to back.
15. At this point you are almost finished. Remove the clip, if you are using one. Carefully proceed through hole 2 from the back to the inside of the book where you began.
16. Open up your pages to the two threads. Tie the threads in a tight double knot, right up against hole 2 where they came through. Trim the threads to about ½" and carefully tuck them back into the stitched spine, hiding them from view.
17. The completed noble binding.

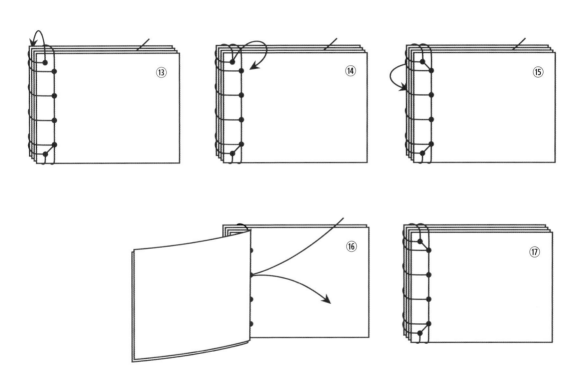

Hemp-Leaf Binding

The hemp-leaf binding is another step past the noble binding in complexity. It too begins in the same way as the Japanese four-hole binding.

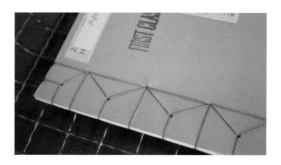

1. This binding requires nine holes. The standard alignment of the four main holes is ⅜" from the edge of the spine. Place the top hole ⅝" from the top edge of the book, place the bottom hole ⅝" from the bottom edge of the book, and place two more holes evenly between the first two holes. The five secondary holes align ³⁄₁₆" from the edge of the spine (halfway between the row of four holes and the spine). Place hole 1a halfway between the top edge of the book and hole 1. Place hole 2a halfway between hole 1 and hole 2. Place hole 3a halfway between hole 2 and 3. Place hole 4a halfway between hole 3 and hole 4. Place hole 4b halfway between hole 4 and the bottom edge of the book. Mark the placement of each hole on a template paper cut to the same size as the top page or cover. You will use a length of thread eight times the height of the spine.

2. You may leave a clip on the fore edge of your pages while you stitch, if you like. Place a small scrap of paper between the clip and your pages to prevent the clip from damaging your pages.

3. To begin, split apart your pages about halfway through the stack. Enter from the inside of the book through hole 2. Leave about 4" of thread inside the book. You will use this section of thread to tie off when you are finished stitching.

4. Place the pages back together in a stack and wrap your thread around the spine, entering from back to front through hole 2.

5. Proceed down the spine through hole 3 from front to back. Wrap the spine and enter hole 3 from front to back again. (Note: It may appear as though you are missing steps as you proceed down the spine. Don't worry; you will complete the missed areas as you work your way back up.)

6. Enter hole 4 from back to front. Wrap the spine and enter hole 4 from back to front again. Then wrap the bottom of the book and enter through hole 4 back to front a third time.

7. At this point, enter hole 4b from front to back. Wrap the spine and enter hole 4b front to back again.

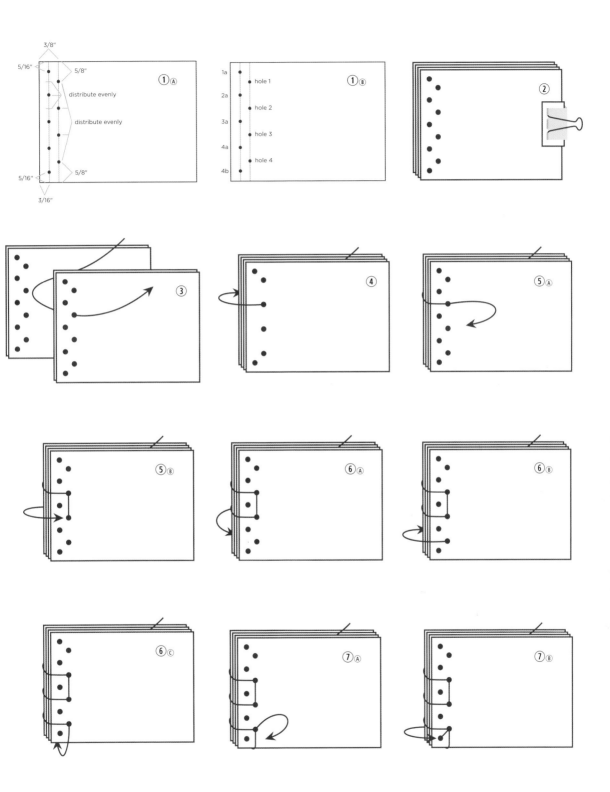

8. Wrap the bottom of the book and enter hole 4b front to back a third time.

9. Complete the corner by entering hole 4 from back to front.

10. Proceed up the spine through hole 4a from front to back.

11. Wrap the spine and enter hole 4a from front to back again.

12. Go down the spine into hole 4 from back to front.

13. Proceed up the spine through hole 3 from front to back.

14. Go down the spine through hole 4a from back to front, then back up the spine through hole 3 from front to back.

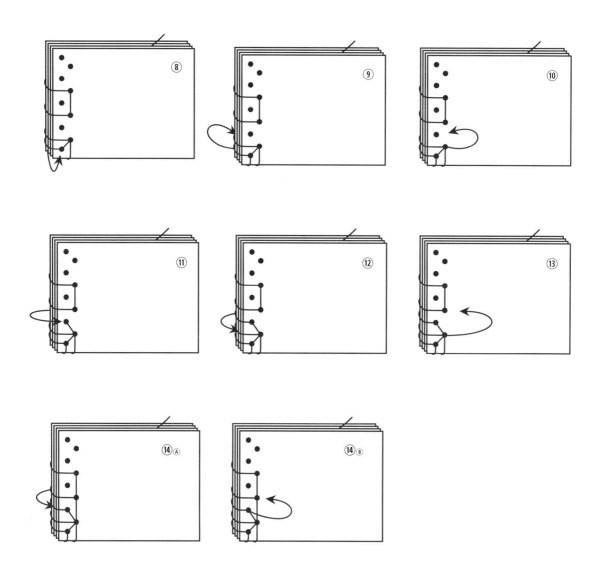

15. Enter hole 3a from back to front. Wrap the spine and enter hole 3a from back to front again.
16. Go down the spine through hole 3 from front to back.
17. Proceed up the spine through hole 2 from back to front.
18. Go down the spine through hole 3a from front to back and proceed up the spine through hole 2 back to front.
19. Proceed up the spine through hole 1 from front to back.
20. Wrap the spine and enter hole 1 from front to back again. Then wrap the top of the book and enter hole 1 from front to back a third time.

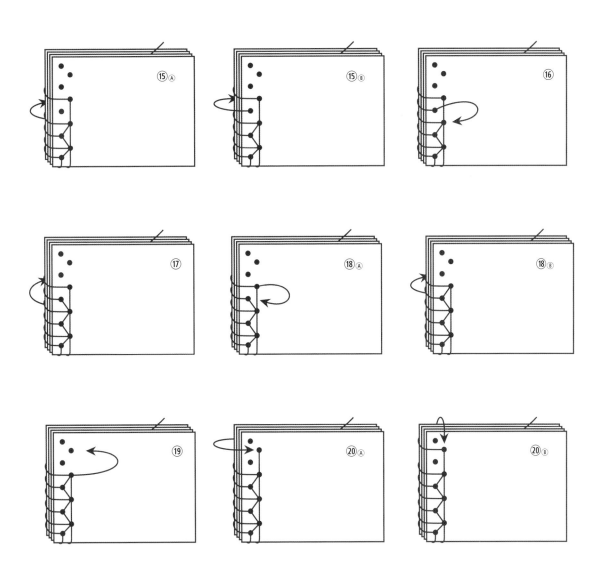

21. Enter hole 1a from back to front. Wrap the spine and enter hole 1a back to front again.
22. Wrap the top of the book and enter hole 1a back to front a third time.
23. Complete the corner by entering hole 1 from front to back.
24. Go down the spine through hole 2a from back to front. Wrap the spine and enter hole 2a from back to front again.
25. Go down the spine through hole 2 from front to back, then proceed up the spine through hole 2a from back to front.
26. Proceed up the spine through hole 1 from front to back.

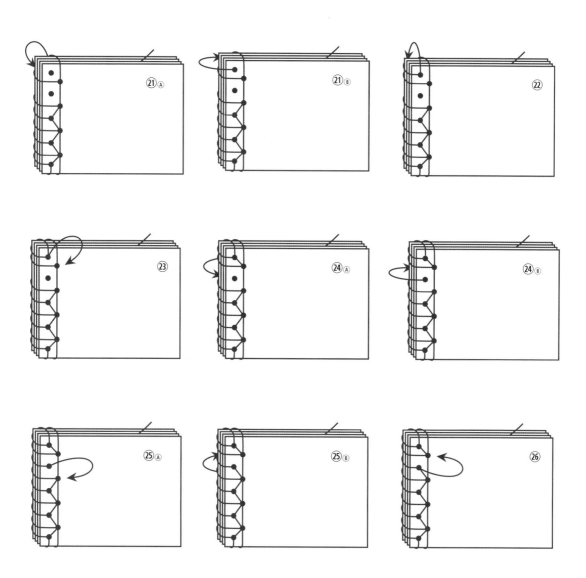

88

27. At this point you are almost finished. Remove the clip, if you are using one. Carefully proceed through hole 2 from the back to the inside of the book where you began.
28. Open up your pages to the two threads. Tie the threads in a tight double knot, right up against hole 2 where they came through. Trim the threads to about ½" and carefully tuck them back into the stitched spine, hiding them from view.
29. The completed hemp-leaf binding.

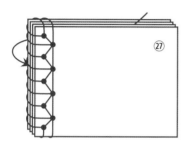

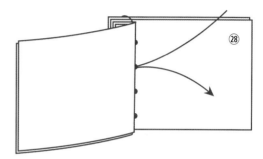

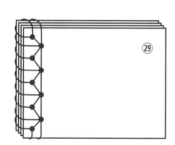

Tortoise-Shell Binding

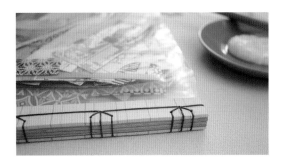

The tortoise-shell binding is slightly different from the other Japanese stab bindings, although it does begin in the same way as the Japanese four-hole binding.

1. This binding requires twelve holes. The standard alignment of the four main holes is ⅜" from the edge of the spine. Place the top hole ⅝" from the top edge of the book, place the bottom hole ⅝" from the bottom edge of the book, and place two more holes evenly between the first two holes. The eight secondary holes align ³⁄₁₆" from the edge of the spine (halfway between the row of four holes and the spine). Place a hole ¼" above and below each main hole. Mark the placement of each hole on a template paper cut to the same size as the top page or cover. You will use a length of thread seven times the height of the spine.

2. You may leave a clip on the fore edge of your pages while you stitch, if you like. Place a small scrap of paper between the clip and your pages to prevent the clip from damaging your pages.

3. To begin, split apart your pages about halfway through the stack. Enter from the inside of the book through hole 2. Leave about 4" of thread inside the book. You will use this section of thread to tie off when you are finished stitching.

4. Place the pages back together in a stack and wrap your thread around the spine, entering hole 2 from back to front.

5. Proceed down the spine through hole 3 from front to back. Wrap the spine and enter hole 3 from front to back again. (Note: It may appear as though you are missing steps as you proceed down the spine. Don't worry; you will complete the missed areas as you work your way back up.)

6. Enter hole 4 from back to front. Wrap the spine and enter hole 4 from back to front again. Then wrap the bottom of the book and enter hole 4 from back to front a third time.

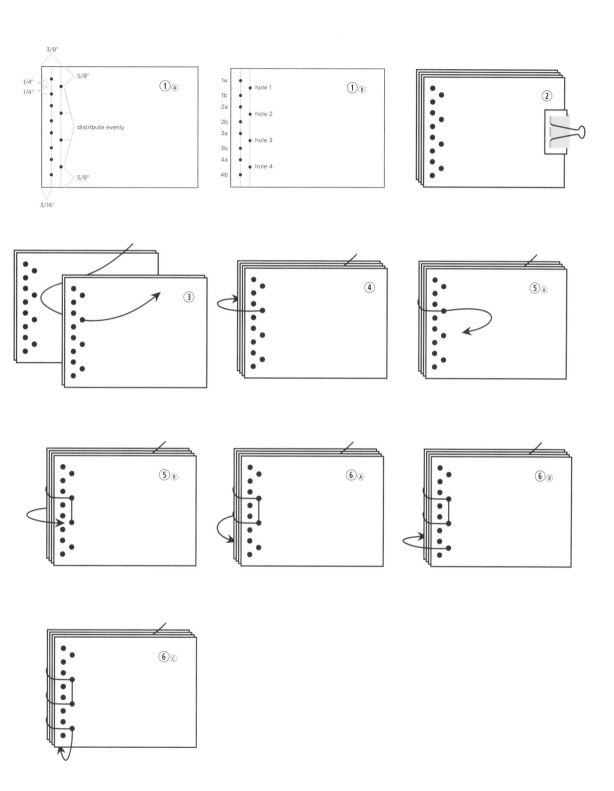

7. From here, enter hole 4b from front to back. Wrap the spine and enter hole 4b from front to back again. Then enter hole 4 from back to front.
8. Proceed up the spine through hole 4a from front to back. Wrap the spine and enter hole 4a from front to back again. Then go back down the spine through hole 4 from back to front.
9. Proceed up the spine through hole 3 from front to back.

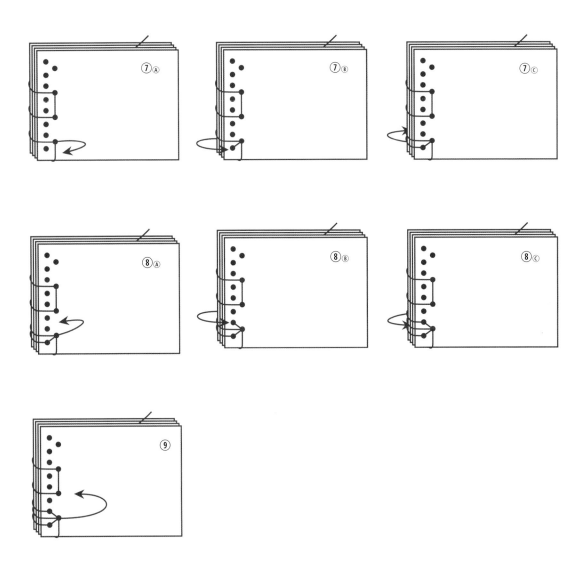

10. Imitate the pattern created through the previous two steps by going down the spine through hole 3b from back to front. Wrap the spine and enter hole 3b from back to front again. Then go back up the spine through hole 3 from front to back.

11. Proceed up the spine through hole 3a from back to front. Wrap the spine and enter hole 3a from back to front again. Then go back down the spine through hole 3 from front to back.

12. Proceed up through hole 2 from back to front.

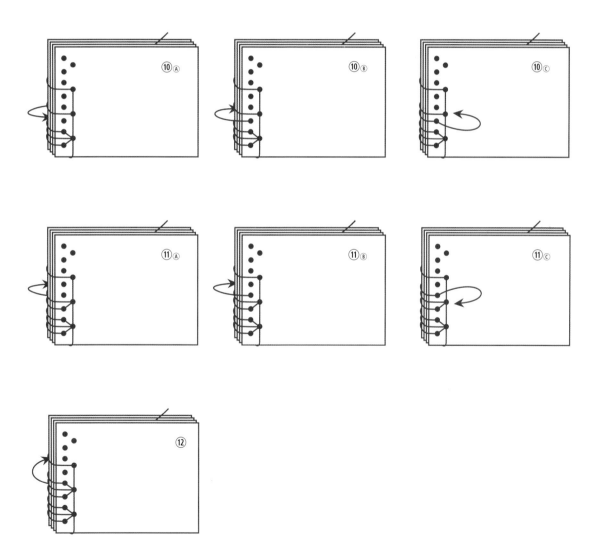

13. Go down the spine through hole 2b from front to back. Wrap the spine and enter hole 2b from front to back again. Then go back up the spine through hole 2 from back to front.

14. Enter hole 2a from front to back. Wrap the spine and enter hole 2a from front to back again. Then go back down the spine through hole 2 from back to front.

15. Proceed up the spine through hole 1 from front to back.

16. Wrap the spine and enter hole 1 from front to back again. Then wrap the top of the book and enter hole 1 from front to back a third time.

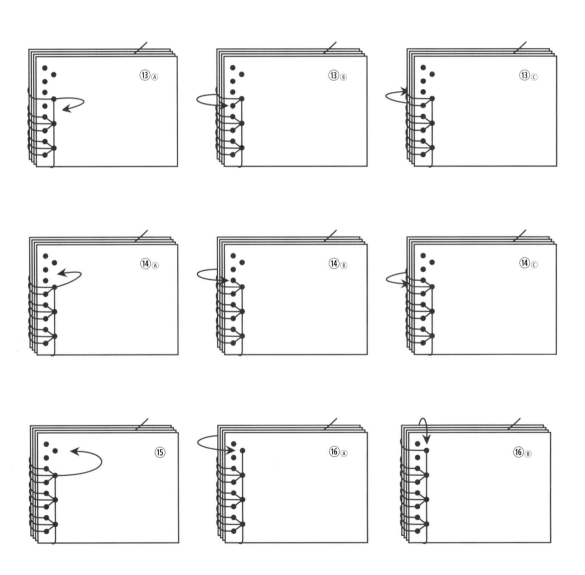

17. Enter hole 1a from back to front. Wrap the spine and enter hole 1a from back to front again. Then go back down the spine through hole 1 from front to back.

18. Go down the spine through hole 1b from back to front. Wrap the spine and enter hole 1b from back to front again. Then go back up the spine through hole 1 from front to back.

19. At this point you are almost finished. Remove the clip, if you are using one.

Carefully proceed through hole 2 from the back to the inside of the book where you began.

20. Open up your pages to the two threads. Tie the threads in a tight double knot, right up against hole 2 where they came through. Trim the threads to about ½" and carefully tuck them back into the stitched spine, hiding them from view.

21. The completed tortoise shell binding.

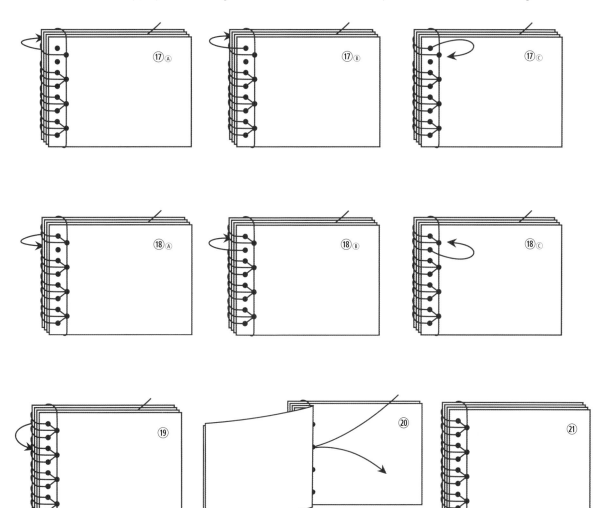

Improvised Japanese Four-Hole Binding

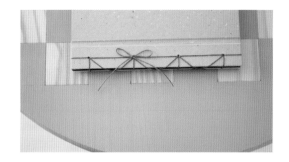

The instructions for this binding direct you to begin and end your stitching from the outside of the cover. If you prefer to hide the knot, you may begin and end the stitching from the inside of the pages, as in the other stab binding instructions (see the Japanese four-hole binding on page 76).

1. This binding requires four holes. The standard alignment of the holes is ⅜" from the edge of the spine. Place the top hole ⅝" from the top edge of the book, place the bottom hole ⅝" from the bottom edge of the book, and place two more holes evenly between the first two holes. Mark the placement of each hole on a template paper cut to the same size as the top page or cover. You will use a length of thread seven times the height of the spine.

2. You may leave a clip on the fore edge of your pages while you stitch, if you like. Place a small scrap of paper between the clip and your pages to prevent the clip from damaging your pages.

3. Begin at hole 2, on the outside of the cover. Leave about 4" of thread at the front of the book. You will use this section of thread to tie off when you are finished stitching. Wrap your needle and thread around the spine, entering hole 2 from back to front.

4. Proceed down the spine through hole 3 from front to back. Wrap the spine and enter hole 3 from front to back again. (Note: It may appear as though you are missing steps as you proceed down the spine. Don't worry; you will complete the missed areas as you work your way back up.)

5. Enter hole 4 from back to front. Wrap the spine and enter hole 4 from back to front again. Then wrap the bottom of the book and enter through hole 4 from back to front a third time.

6. Proceed up the spine through hole 3 from front to back, up the spine again through hole 2 back to front, and then up the spine a third time through hole 1 from front to back.

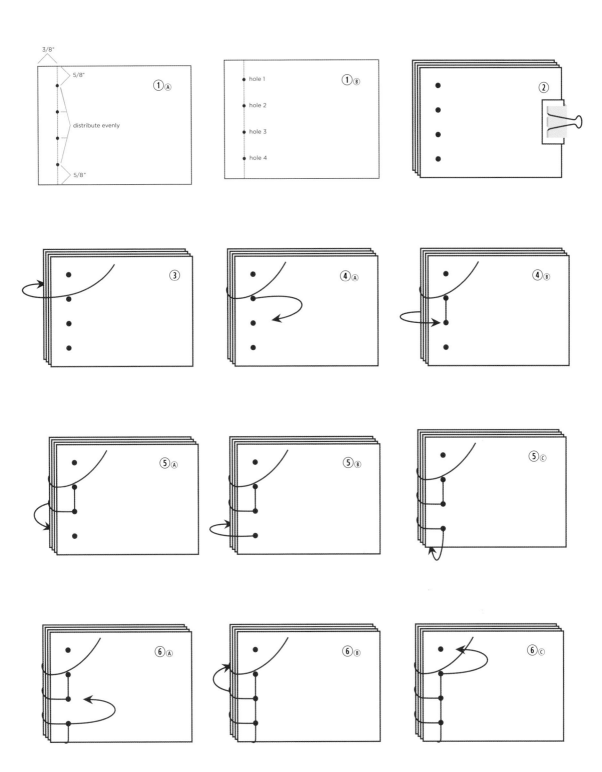

7. Wrap the spine and enter hole 1 from front to back again. Then wrap the top of the book and enter hole 1 from front to back a third time.
8. Enter hole 2 from back to front.
9. Wrap around and down the spine. Enter hole 3 from back to front.

10. Wrap around and down the spine. Enter hole 4 from back to front.
11. Wrap around and up the spine. Enter hole 3 from the back.
12. Wrap around and up the spine. Enter hole 2 from back to front.
13. Wrap around and up the spine. Enter hole 1 from back to front.

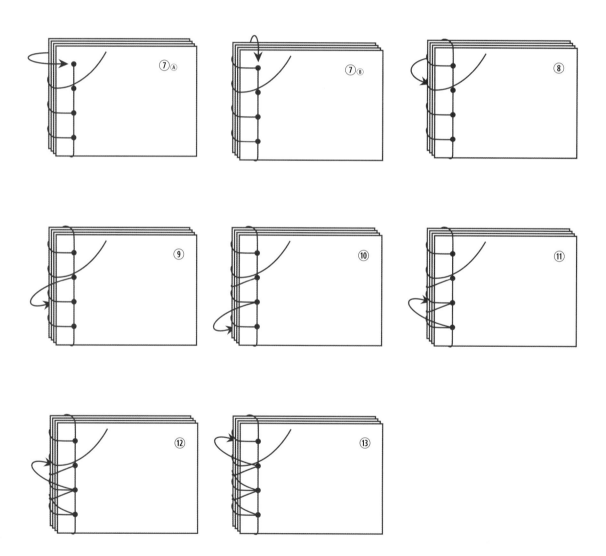

14. Wrap around and down the spine. Enter hole 2 from back to front.

15. Your thread is now at hole 2, where you began.

16. Tie the threads in a tight double knot, right up against hole 2. Tie a bow and trim the extra thread. The completed improvised Japanese four-hole binding.

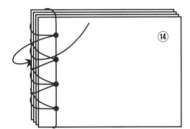

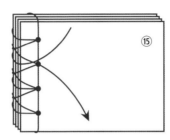

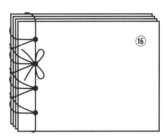

Yamato Binding

The Yamato binding is the simplest of all the stab bindings. It requires only two holes, and the threads tie at the outside of the cover.

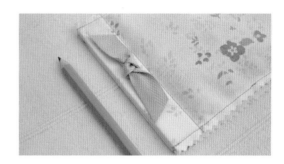

1. This binding requires two holes. The standard alignment of the holes is ½" from the edge of the spine. Divide the length of the spine into three parts. Place the holes at the two points dividing the three parts, evenly distributing the two holes between the top and bottom of the page. Mark the placement of each hole on a template paper cut to the same size as the top page or cover. You will use a length of thread three times the height of the spine.

2. You may leave a clip on the fore edge of your pages while you stitch, if you like. Place a small scrap of paper between the clip and your pages to prevent the clip from damaging your pages.

3. To begin, enter from the outside of the front cover through hole 1. Leave about half of the thread at the front of the book. You will use this section of thread to tie off when you are finished stitching.

4. Enter hole 2 from back to front.

5. Tie the threads in a tight double knot centered between the holes. Tie a bow, and trim the extra thread. The completed Yamato binding.

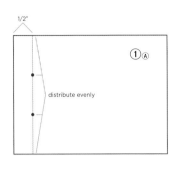

1/2"

distribute evenly

①Ⓐ

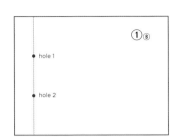

● hole 1

● hole 2

①Ⓑ

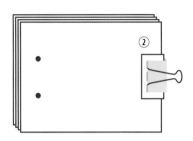

②

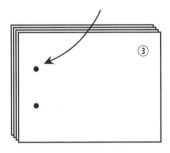

③

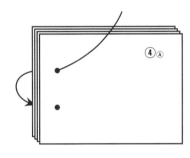

④Ⓐ

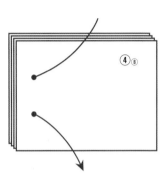

④Ⓑ

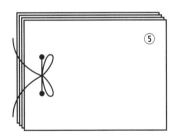

⑤

Account Book Binding

The account book binding is another simple stab binding. It features long threads that extend from the top of the book.

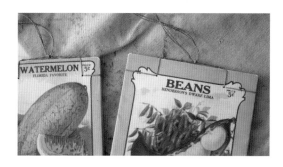

1. This binding requires two holes. The standard alignment of the holes is ½" from the edge of the spine. Divide the length of the spine into three parts. Place the holes at the two points dividing the three parts, evenly distributing the two holes between the top and bottom of the page. Mark the placement of the holes on a template paper cut to the same size as the top page or cover. You will use two separate threads, one for each hole. Cut each thread to five times the height of the spine.

2. You may leave a clip on the fore edge of your pages while you stitch, if you like. Place a small scrap of paper between the clip and your pages to prevent the clip from damaging your pages.

3. To begin, enter from the outside of the front cover through hole 1. Leave about one third of the thread at the front of the book. You will use this section of thread to tie off when you are finished stitching.

4. Wrap the top of the book and enter hole 1 from front to back again.

5. Tie the ends of the thread in a tight double knot centered over the spine and directly across from hole 1.

6. With the second thread, enter from the outside of the front cover through hole 2. Leave about one third of the thread at the front of the book to tie off.

7. Wrap the bottom of the book and enter hole 2 from front to back again.

8. Tie the ends of the thread in a tight double knot centered over the spine and directly across from hole 2.

9. Twist each pair of threads tightly together. Tie the pairs of twisted threads together in a double knot centered over the spine and directly between the holes. Trim extra thread to a desired length. The completed account book binding.

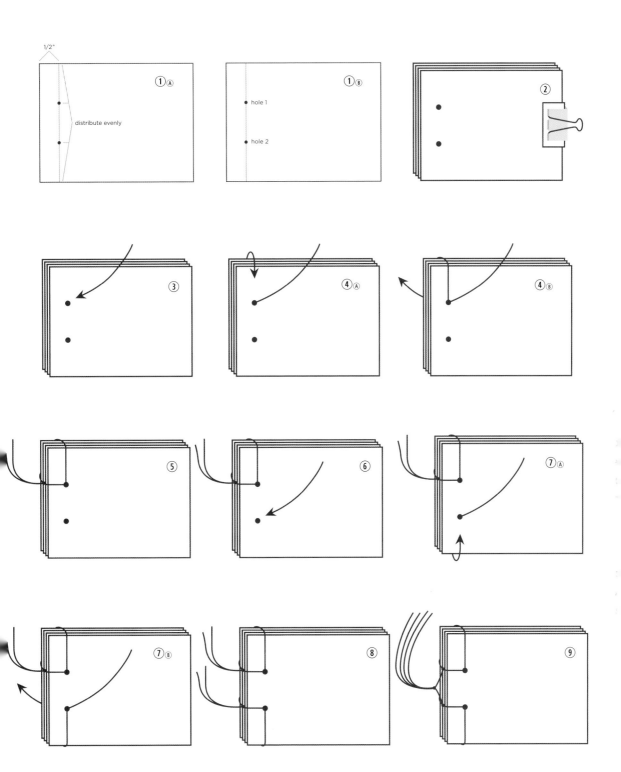

1/2"

distribute evenly

① Ⓐ

hole 1

hole 2

① Ⓑ

②

③

④ Ⓐ

④ Ⓑ

⑤

⑥

⑦ Ⓐ

⑦ Ⓑ

⑧

⑨

Ledger Binding

The ledger binding uses pages that are folded in half. The binding is sewn along the fold at the spine.

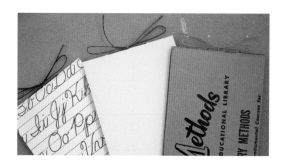

1. This binding requires three holes. The standard alignment of the holes is right along the edge of the spine. Place hole 2 directly in the center of the spine. Center hole 1 between hole 2 and the top of the page. Center hole 3 between hole 2 and the bottom of the page. Mark the placement of each hole on a template paper cut to the same size as the inside pages. You will use a length of thread three times the height of the spine.

2. To begin, enter from the outside of the spine through hole 2 to the inside of the book. Leave about one third of the thread at the outside of the book. You will use this section of thread to tie off when you are finished sewing.

3. Travel up along the inside of the book along the fold and exit at hole 1. Go down the outside of the spine and enter hole 3 to the inside of the book.

4. Travel up along the inside of the book along the fold and exit at hole 2.

5. Make sure each end of the thread is on opposite sides of the thread that runs along the spine. Tie the threads in a double knot centered over hole 2, securing the thread that runs along the spine in the knot. Trim the extra thread to desired length. The completed ledger binding.

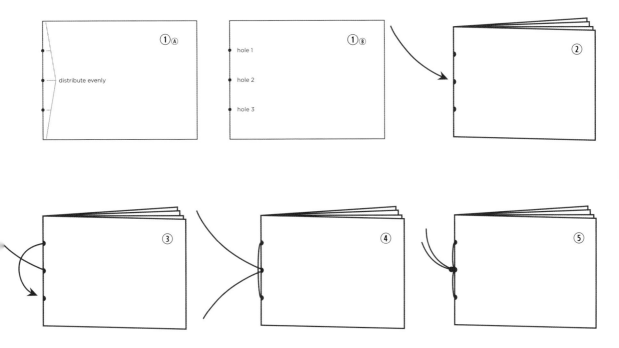

distribute evenly

hole 1

hole 2

hole 3

STEP-BY-STEP INSTRUCTIONS

Bon Appétit Place Card

See photographs on pages 10–11.

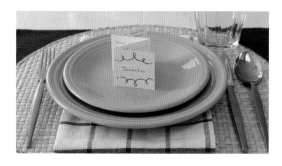

Finished Size
2" square

Tools
Metal ruler
Craft knife
Cutting mat or protective cutting surface
Bone folder
Book press or heavy stack of books

Materials
Card stock: 1 piece, cut to 8" x 2"

Instructions

1. Trim your papers to size with a metal ruler and craft knife.
2. Fold the card stock in half, right to left. Burnish. Fold each end back toward the first folded edge. Burnish. You will have three folds and four panels.
3. If you find the accordion to be too springy, press it flat in a folded position for a few hours.
4. Write the name of your guest on the front. Fill out the inside with the menu; you can also include quotes or pictures. Use pens, colored pencils, stamps, and stickers to decorate the place card to match your table decor.

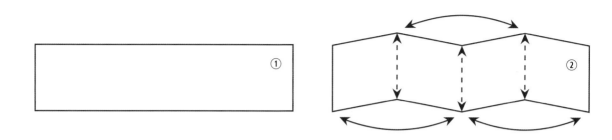

Read and Write Bookmark Book

See photograph on pages 12–13.

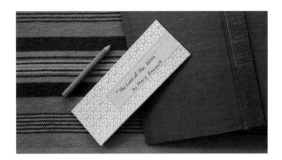

Finished Size
2¼" x 6"

Tools
Metal ruler
Craft knife
Awl or pencil
Paste, glue, or glue stick
Small paste brush (if using paste or glue)
Waxed paper to protect work surface
Book press or heavy stack of books

Materials
Text weight or lightweight paper: 1 piece, cut to
    14" x 5⅞"
Cover stock paper: 2 pieces, cut to 2¼" x 6"
Thin, decorative end paper: 2 pieces, cut to
    2½" x 5⅞"
Title strip (either a paper scrap or a sticker label):
    About 1" x 4"

Instructions

1. Notice the paper grain of your text weight paper. Place the direction of the paper grain top to bottom, parallel to where the accordion folds will be. Trim your papers to size with a metal ruler and craft knife.

2. Using the ruler and awl (or pencil), measure and mark the placement of the accordion folds along the bottom of the text weight paper at these measurements: ½", 4¾", 9", 13¼".

3. Fold the text paper left to right along the fold marks. You will have four folds.

4. Match folded edge to folded edge to create the reverse accordion folds. You will have three more folds.

5. Apply a thin layer of glue along the edge of the back side of one endpaper. Adhere the end paper to the short flap of text paper. Repeat with the other endpaper and text paper flap.

6. Fold back the outside edge of each endpaper so that each is the same size as the accordion folded text paper. Paste the flaps down.

7. Apply paste to the back side of the front endpaper. Carefully place the end paper, centered, on the inside of the front cover. Repeat this process, adhering the back endpaper to the inside of the back cover. Be careful to match the front and back so that the covers are straight.

8. Place a small piece of wax paper between the covers and text paper and close the book. Place a piece of wax paper around the cover. Press flat.

9. Paste the title strip to the front cover, ⅛" from the top of the book and centered left to right.

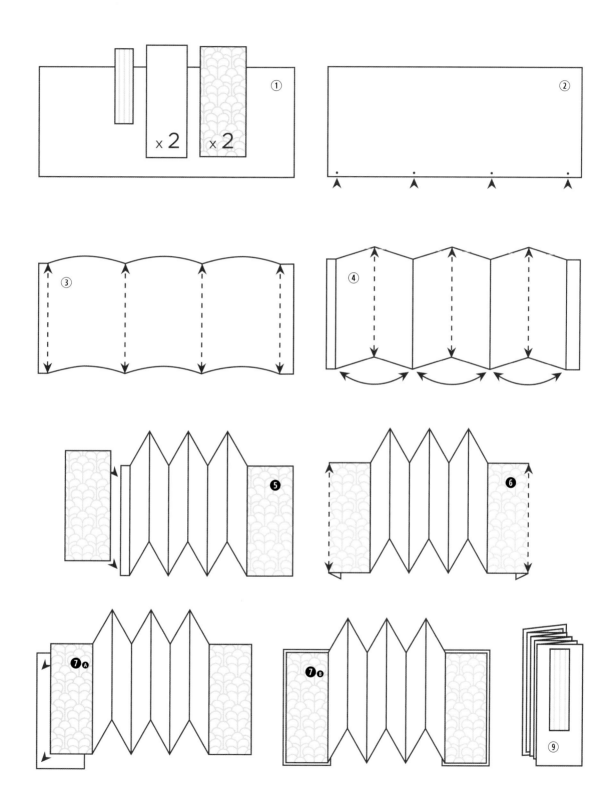

Two-or-Three-View Picture

See photograph on page 14.

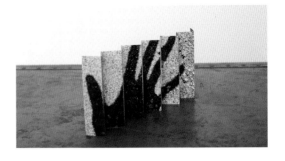

2, 3) for the three-view picture. Press until completely dry.

6. Once dry, fold the two- or three- view picture as shown and display.

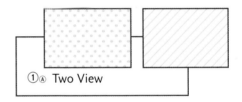

① Ⓐ Two View

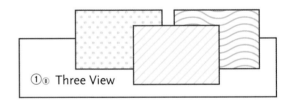

① Ⓑ Three View

Instructions

1. Trim your papers to size with a metal ruler and craft knife.
2. Cut each photo into vertical strips, just a bit narrower than 1" (about 1⁵⁄₁₆"). You may have a small amount of each photo left over. This will leave space for the card stock to fold.
3. Score the card stock vertically, leaving 1" between each score line.
4. Fold along each scored line. Burnish.
5. Paste the photo strips onto the card stock between the folds, leaving a bit of space between each strip. Alternate the photo strips (1, 2, 1, 2, 1, 2, 1, 2, 1, 2, 1, 2) for the two-view picture. Alternate the photo strips (1, 2, 3, 1, 2, 3, 1, 2, 3, 1, 2, 3, 1, 2, 3, 1,

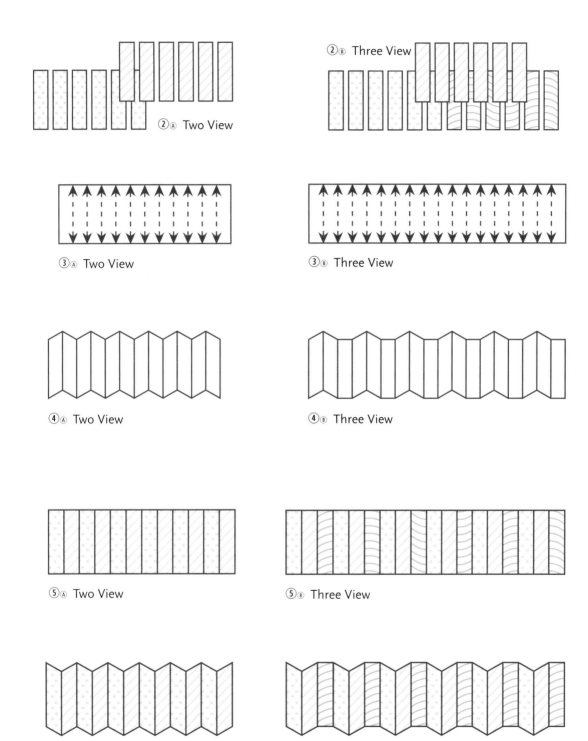

②Ⓐ Two View

②Ⓑ Three View

③Ⓐ Two View

③Ⓑ Three View

④Ⓐ Two View

④Ⓑ Three View

⑤Ⓐ Two View

⑤Ⓑ Three View

⑥Ⓐ Two View

⑥Ⓑ Three View

Unfolding Flower Notes

See photograph on page 15.

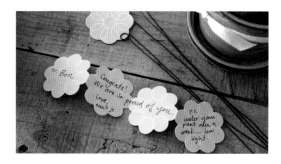

Finished Size

2" in diameter

Tools

Metal ruler
Craft knife
Cutting mat or protective cutting surface
Pencil
Scissors
Bone folder
Needle nose pliers
Wire clippers

Materials

Text weight paper: 1 piece, cut to 8" x 2"
Template paper: 2" x 2"
Floral pick or thick wire (19 gauge steel wire):
    1 piece, cut to 12"

Instructions

1. Trim your papers to size with a metal ruler and craft knife.
2. Create a flower pattern from the template paper. Either draw your own flower design or trace the flower template on page 115. Make sure that the design touches the edge of the paper on both the left and right sides. Cut out the flower template.
3. Fold the text weight paper in half right to left. Burnish. Fold each end back toward the first folded edge. Burnish. You will have three folds and four panels.
4. Place the flower template on top of the folded accordion. Trace the template directly onto the front with a pencil. Make sure that the flower extends past the folds at the left and right sides, so that you don't cut off the folds. Cut along the pencil lines with scissors, through all four layers.
5. When you open up the book, each flower will be attached to one another at the sides.
6. To make your own wire floral pick, clip a piece of steel wire to size. Pinch one end of the wire at the tip with the needle nose pliers. Wrap the extending wire around the tip of the pliers twice. Pull the wire off of the pliers. Use the pliers to bend the wire down from the little loop. Cut the wire to desired length.
7. Place the paper flower book between the little loops in the wire and poke the other end down into the soil of a potted plant.

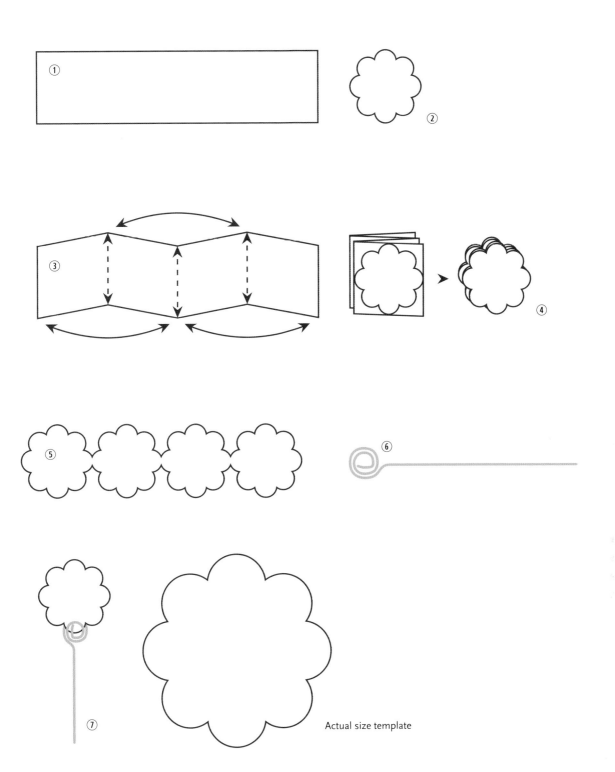

Actual size template

Wish-You-Were-Here Postcard Journal

See photograph on page 18.

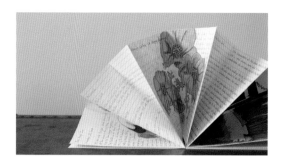

3. Apply glue to the back of one folded paper in a ⅛" strip along the open edge. Adhere to the back of a second folded paper, aligning the open edges. Repeat until all 10 papers are attached to one another. Wrap in waxed paper and press until dry.
4. Apply glue to the back side of the first page of the accordion. Center the page within the back side of the front cover. Smooth.
5. Apply glue to the back of the last page of the accordion. Center the page within the back side of the back cover. Smooth.
6. Press flat until dry.

Instructions

1. Trim your papers to size with a metal ruler and craft knife.
2. Fold each paper in half left to right. Burnish.

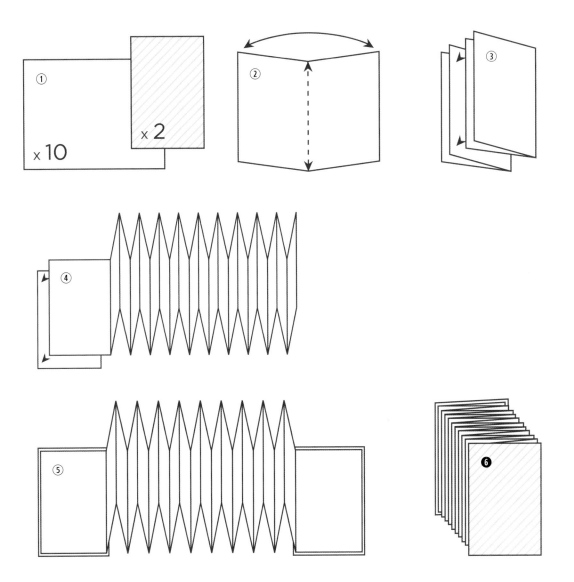

Travel Photo Album

See photograph on page 19.

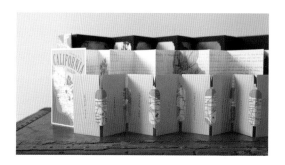

Instructions

1. Notice the paper grain of your medium weight paper. Place the direction of the paper grain top to bottom, parallel to where the accordion folds will be. Piece as many pieces together as you need to reach 50" by applying paste to the end of a paper and overlapping papers by about ¼".

2. Trim your papers and book board to size with a metal ruler and craft knife.

3. Using the ruler and awl (or pencil), measure and mark every other accordion fold along the bottom of the medium weight paper at these measurements: 5", 15", 25", 35", 45".

4. Fold the paper in, left to right, along the fold marks. Burnish. You will have five folds.

5. Match folded edge to folded edge to create the reverse accordion folds. Burnish. You will have four more folds.

6. Place the map papers face down. Place a piece of book board in the very center of each map paper and trace with a pencil.

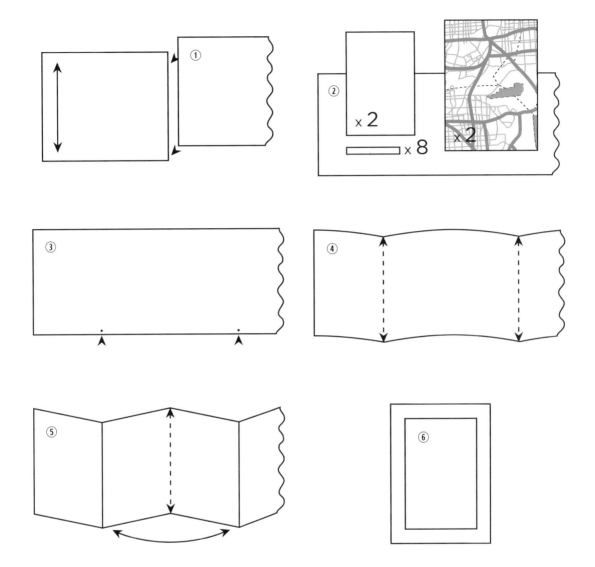

7. Trim all corners from the map papers, leaving ¼" beyond each corner of the penciled-in boxes.

8. Apply a thin layer of paste to the back side of one trimmed map paper. Place one of the book board pieces directly inside of the box that you drew. Flip the glued board over onto a piece of waxed paper and smooth to remove air bubbles. Flip it again.

Fold over the edges, long sides first and short sides last. Smooth. Press until dry. Repeat with the other cover.

9. Make two marks on the inside of the back cover halfway between the top and bottom edges and ½" in from each side. Paste one end of each ribbon at the two marks inside the back cover. Press until dry.

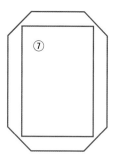
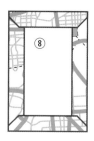
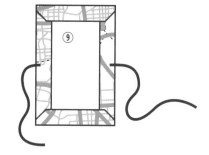

10. Apply a thin layer of paste to the back side of the first accordion panel. Place it centered within the inside of the front cover. Smooth. Press until dry.
11. Repeat step 10, adhering the back accordion panel to the inside of the back cover.
12. Use a pencil to mark the placement of the photos on each page. Place four photo corners to hold a 4" x 6" photo on each page. Fill the album with eight favorite photos. Adhere photo labels 1/8" below each photo.
13. Wrap the ribbons around and tie in the front to keep the album closed.

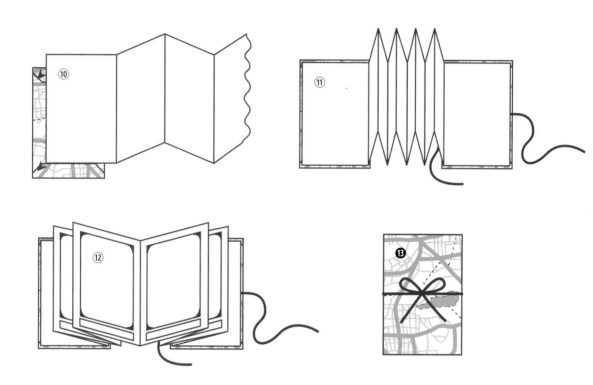

Tiny Souvenir Book

See photograph on pages 20–21.

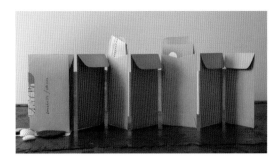

Instructions

1. Trim your paper hinges to size with a metal ruler and craft knife. If you like, you can round the corners of each piece of map paper.

2. Draw light pencil marks on the face of each envelope for placement of the hinges. Draw two lines from top to bottom, one ⅜" in from the left side and another ⅜" in from the right side. Mark another two lines, one ¾" up from the bottom of the envelope, and another 1" down from the top.

3. Apply glue to the back of a piece of hinge paper. On a piece of waxed paper, line the hinge up within the pencil marks between two envelopes. The hinge will connect the right side of one envelope to the left side of another envelope. There will be about a ¼" gap between the envelopes. Smooth. Repeat until all envelopes are connected to one another. Press until dry. Erase the pencil lines after the glue is completely dry.

4. Carefully fold the envelopes into an accordion, lining up the envelopes with one another. Burnish.

5. Use the book to hold objects such as tickets and small stones. Write the contents of each envelope on the front. Use a rubber band to hold the folded book together.

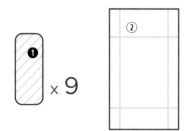 × 9

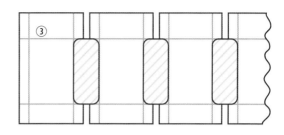

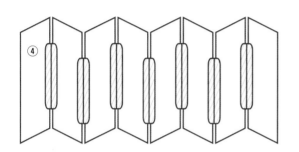

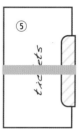

tickets

Idea File

See photograph on page 24.

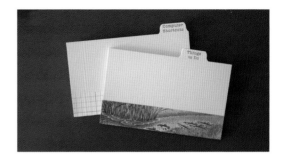

Finished Size

3 3/8" x 5" (including the tab)

Tools

Paste, glue, or glue stick
Small paste brush (if using paste or glue)
Waxed paper to protect work surface
Metal ruler
Craft knife
Cutting mat or protective cutting surface
Awl or pencil
Bone folder
Book press or heavy stack of books

Materials

Tabbed index card guides: 2 cards, each 3" x 5"
Text weight paper: 25" x 4 15/16"
Text weight decorative paper to cover spine: 2" x 5"

Instructions

1. Glue pieces of text weight paper together, overlapping them by 1/8", until you have a 25" long paper.
2. Trim your papers to size with a metal ruler and craft knife.
3. Using the ruler and awl (or pencil), measure and mark the accordion folds along the bottom of the text weight paper at these measurements: 3/4", 6 5/8", 12 1/2", 18 3/8", 24 1/4".
4. Fold the text paper toward the back, along the fold marks. Burnish. You will have five folds.
5. Match folded edge to folded edge to create the reverse accordion folds. Burnish. You will have four more folds and a total of eight pages each 2 15/16" with a 3/4" flap on each end.
6. Apply a thin layer of glue to the front flap. Line up the folded text weight paper with the inside of the front cover along the spine. Adhere the flap to the inside of the front cover. Smooth.

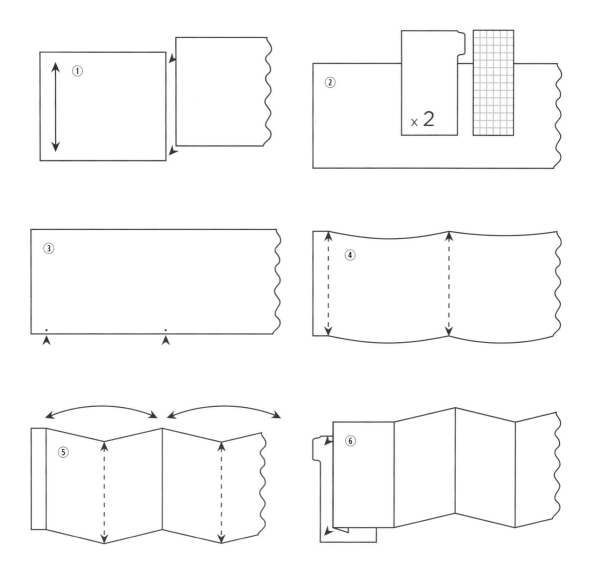

7. Repeat step 6, adhering the back flap to the back cover. Press until dry.
8. Fold the 2" x 5" decorative paper in half lengthwise, pattern face out.

9. Apply a thin layer of glue to the back of the decorative paper. Line up the spine of the front cover, face down, along the center fold of the decorative paper. Adhere. Flip and smooth from the front side.

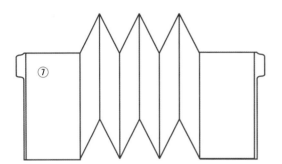

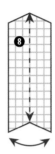

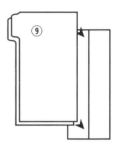

10. Flip again, with the front cover face down. Pull the remaining half of the decorative paper around the spine and adhere it to the back cover. Smooth. Press until dry.

11. Repeat steps 1 through 10 until you have a set of tabbed books. Keep your collection of books in a 3" x 5" office box or recipe box.

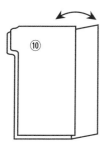

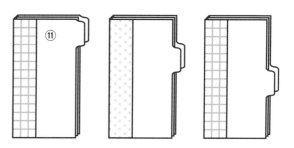

Sketch, Jot, Journal

See photograph on page 25.

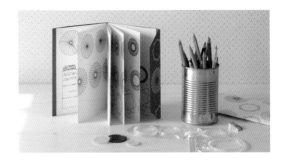

Finished Size
5" x 7"

Tools
Paste, glue, or glue stick
Small paste brush (if using paste or glue)
Waxed paper to protect work surface
Metal ruler
Craft knife
Cutting mat or protective cutting surface
Awl or pencil
Bone folder
Book press or heavy stack of books

Materials
Card stock: 12" x 7"
Drawing paper: 46¼" x 7"

Instructions

1. Glue pieces of drawing paper together, overlapping ⅛", until you have a 46¼" long paper.
2. Trim your paper and cover to size with a metal ruler and craft knife.
3. Using the ruler and awl (or pencil), measure and mark the accordion folds along the bottom of the drawing paper at these measurements: ⅝", 9⅝", 18⅝", 27⅝", 36⅝", 45⅝".
4. Fold the drawing paper facing toward the back along the fold marks. You will have six folds. Burnish.
5. Match folded edge to folded edge to create the reverse accordion folds. You will have five more folds and ten 4½" pages with a ⅝" flap on each end. Burnish.
6. Lay the cover on your work surface horizontally and face down. Use the bone folder and ruler to score the cover paper from top to bottom, 2" from the right edge and again 7" from the right edge. This will create two 5" panels and one 2" flap. Fold the cover at the scored lines and burnish.

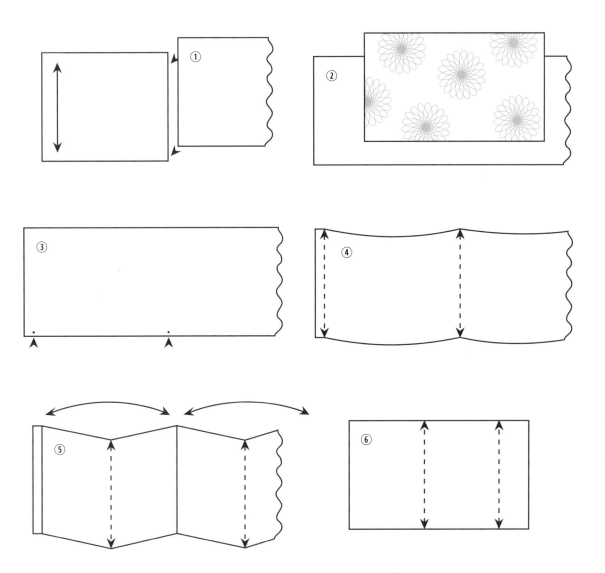

7. Use a pencil to mark each corner of the cover flap. Mark 1½" away from the corner toward the fold and mark 1" away from the corner toward the center. Draw a straight line between the two marks at each corner.

To mark the slit for the flap, make two pencil marks 1½" in from the left edge of the cover. Mark once ⅝" in from the top and again ⅝" in from the bottom. Draw a straight line between the two marks.

8. Use a metal ruler and craft knife to cut along the pencil marks. Check your measurements by tucking the flap into the slit.

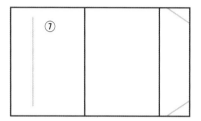

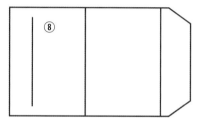

9. Apply a thin layer of glue to the front flap of the accordion folded drawing paper. With the pages folded into place, tuck the pages into the cover, gently nesting them down into the fold of the spine. There will be a small gap between the fold of the cover and the pages. Adhere the flap to the inside of the front cover. Smooth.

10. Repeat step 9, adhering the back flap to the back cover. Press until dry.

11. Tuck the flap in to close the book.

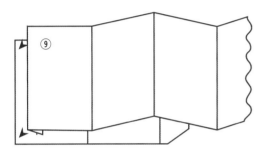 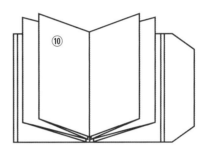 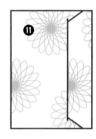

Tag Notebook

See photograph on page 28.

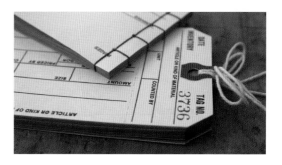

Finished Size
3⅛" x 6¼" x ¼"

Tools
Metal ruler
Craft knife
Cutting mat or protective cutting surface
Pencil
Bulldog clip
Awl
Needle
Scissors

Materials
Manila tags: 2 tags, each 3⅛" x 6 ¼"
Kraft paper: 30 pages, cut to cover size, 3⅛" x 6 ¼"
Template paper: Cut to cover size, 3⅛" x 6¼"
Waxed linen thread: 22"
Cotton string: Two pieces, each 12"

Instructions

1. If the tags have strings attached, remove them and save them for later.
2. Trim your papers to size with a metal ruler and craft knife. If you are using a roll of brown kraft paper, roll it in the opposite direction and secure it with a rubber band for a few hours to remove the curl before trimming your papers.
3. Cut a piece of scrap paper to the cover size to serve as a hole punch template. Mark a line ⅜" from the spine edge. Mark four holes along this line, one ⅝" from the top, another ⅝" from the bottom, and the third and fourth evenly distributed between the first two holes.
4. Carefully line up the covers and inside pages. Clip with a bulldog clip along the fore edge. Place a small scrap of paper between the clips and the covers to prevent the clip from damaging the covers.
5. Line up the template at the spine and punch holes in the stack of pages at the marks.
6. Stitch the spine following the instructions for the Japanese four-hole binding on page 76–79.
7. If the tags have clipped corners at the fore edge, carefully trim the extra kraft paper at the corners to match the covers.
8. Add a string to each tag. To do this, fold one string in half. Thread the looped end through the hole in the tag. Pull the two ends of the string through the loop until snug. Repeat with the other tag and string. Trim the strings, if needed.
9. Tie the strings together.

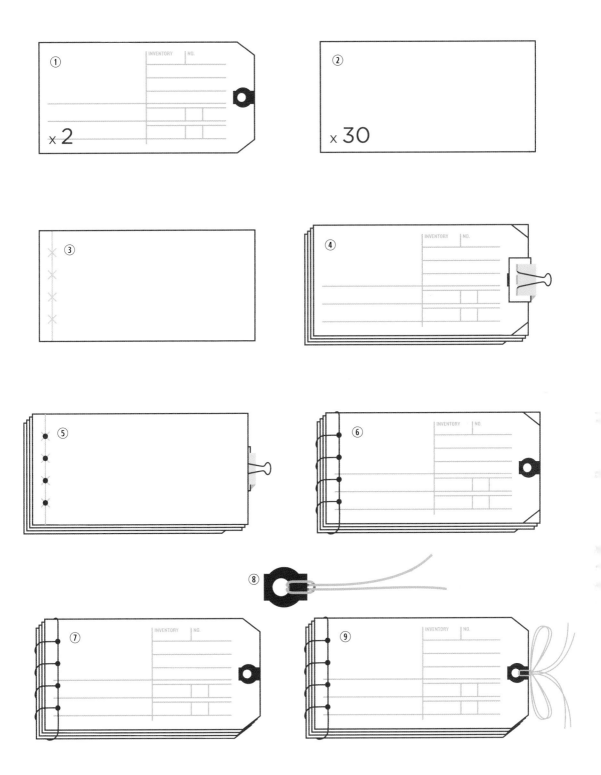

Return-to-Sender Mail Book

See photograph page 29.

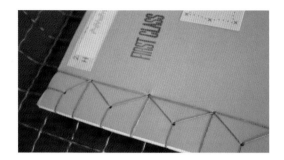

Finished Size

6½" x 9½" x 3/16"

Tools

Metal ruler
Craft knife
Cutting mat or protective cutting surface
Pencil
Bulldog clip
Awl
Needle
Scissors
Paste and paste brush or glue stick
Waxed paper

Materials

Catalog envelope with flap: 2 envelopes, each 6½" x 9½"
Text weight paper: 30 pages, cut to 6½" x 9¼"
Template paper: Cut to cover size, 6½" x 9½"
Text weight paper for mailing label: 1½" x 6"
Waxed linen thread: 55"

Instructions

1. Trim your papers to size with a metal ruler and craft knife. The height of the inside pages should be the same height as the mailer. The width should be the same as the width of the mailer minus ¼" (with flap closed).

2. Cut a piece of scrap paper to the cover size to serve as a hole punch template. Mark two lines, one 1" from the spine edge, and another ½" from the spine edge. Mark four holes along the inner line, one 1" from the top, another 1" from the bottom,

and the third and fourth evenly distributed between the first two holes. Mark five holes along the outer line, each one evenly distributed between the hole marks on the first line.

3. Carefully align the inside pages between the covers, with the bottom of each envelope at the spine. The flap of each envelope will face inward toward the pages. Align and clip with a bulldog clip along the fore edge. Place a small scrap of paper between the clip and the covers to prevent the clip from damaging the covers.

4. Use the template to punch the holes.

5. Stitch the spine following the instructions for the hemp-leaf binding on page 84–89.

6. Adhere the address label to the center of the front cover.

7. Before mailing, fold the flap of the front cover around the fore edge and adhere to the back of the book. The recipient can open the book by cutting open the sealed end. To mail the book a second time, just wrap the flap from the back cover around to the front and repost.

8. Be sure to check postal rates before mailing your book.

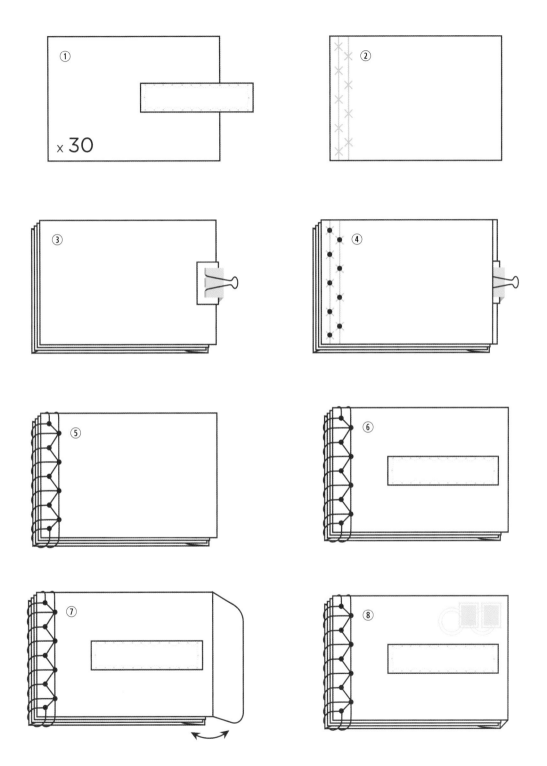

Recycle Bin Book

See photograph on page 30.

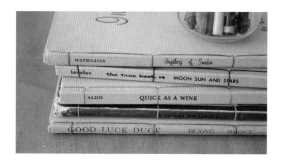

See photograph on page 30.

Finished Size
Varies, will be the size of your hardcover book

Tools
Metal ruler
Craft knife
Cutting mat or protective cutting surface
Waxed paper
Small glue brush
Paste or glue
Bone folder
Book press or heavy stack of books
Bulldog clip
Rubber band
Pencil
Awl and / or hole punch
Tapestry needle

Materials
Used, hardcover book: About ⅜" thick
Text weight endpaper: 2" wide and the height of
   the endpaper already glued to the inside of the
   covers
Text weight mixed papers: About 40 pages cut
   to the cover height minus 1/16" and the cover
   width minus ¼"
Waxed linen thread: 5x the cover height

Instructions

1. Choose a used, hardcover book. Measure the height and width and use these measurements to determine the size of the pages.

2. Trim your mixed papers and endpaper to size with a metal ruler and craft knife.

3. Use a craft knife to carefully remove the pages from the hardcover book. Cut right along the fold of the paper that attaches the pages to the front cover. Be

careful to not cut into the cover! Repeat to detach the back cover.

4. Open up the book cover, and lay it flat, facing up, on your work surface. Apply paste to the back of the endpaper. Center the endpaper over the inside of the spine of the book and paste it down. Smooth. Press until dry.

5. Align the inside pages and clip with a bulldog clip along the fore edge. Place a small scrap of paper between the clip and the pages to prevent the clip from damaging the pages. Slip the book block into the cover to make sure that the pages are the right size. The pages should be about the same height as the cover and about ⅛" less than the width of the cover. Remove the clipped pages from the cover.

6. Lay the book block flat on a piece of waxed paper. Slide the book so that the spine is just off of the edge of your work surface. Brush a thin layer of glue along the spine. Let the glue dry completely. Remove the bulldog clip.

7. Place the book block back inside the cover. Place the spine snugly against the spine of the cover. Clip or rubber band the cover to hold everything in place. If you are using a bulldog clip, place a small scrap of paper between the clip and the cover to prevent the clip from damaging the cover.

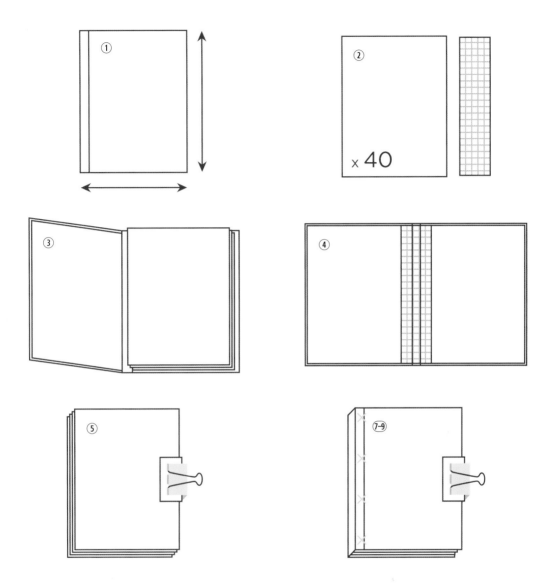

8. Use a pencil and ruler to mark four holes right along the hinge, just to the left of the front cover. Mark one hole ⅝" from the top, another ⅝" from the bottom, and the third and fourth evenly distributed between the first two holes.

9. Use an awl to lightly mark a hole at each pencil mark, marking the front cover and the top page of the book block.

10. Unclip and remove the book block from the cover. Lay the cover open flat, face down. Mark four holes on the back cover, right along the hinge, equal to the marks on the front cover. Punch holes at the marks in both the front and back covers.

11. Use the four small marks as guides to punch all the way through the book block.

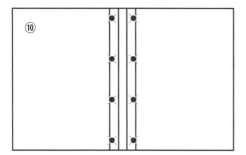

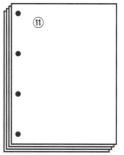

12. Place the punched book block back in place within the punched covers.

13. Stitch the spine following the instructions for the Japanese four-hole binding on pages 76–79.

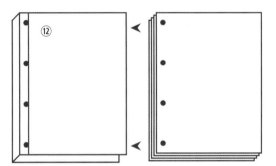

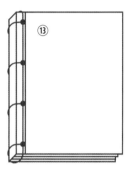

Peek-a-Book

See photograph on page 31.

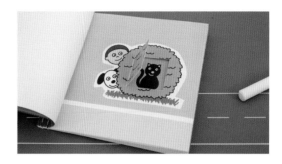

Finished Size

5" x 5" x ¼"

Tools

Metal ruler
Craft knife
Cutting mat or protective surface
Bone folder
Pencil
Paste, glue, or glue stick
Small paste brush (if using paste or glue)
Waxed paper to protect work surface
Book press or heavy stack of books
Bulldog clip
Hole punch (heavy duty for punching through book board)
Hammer
Tapestry needle

Materials

Medium weight paper: 10 to 15 pieces cut to 10" x 5"
Template paper: 5" x 5"
Decorative cover paper: 2 pieces cut to 5¾" x 6"
Endpaper for inside of covers: 2 pieces cut to 4¹⁵⁄₁₆" x 4¹⁵⁄₁₆"
Title strip: Optional
Thread or string: 30"

Instructions

1. Trim your papers to size with a metal ruler and craft knife. For the inside pages, choose papers that have interesting images on them or create images of your own.

2. Use a metal ruler and bone folder to score along the edges of each decorative cover paper. Score a line ½" in from the top, bottom and fore edge. Score a line ¼" in from the spine edge.

3. Lay each decorative paper face down, and fold the edges in along the scored lines. Burnish.

4. Trim the excess paper at each corner.

5. Lay one cover face down onto a piece of waxed paper. Apply a thin layer of paste to all four flaps. Center the endpaper and adhere to the flaps. Burnish. Press until dry. Repeat with the other cover.

6. Fold each 10" x 5" page in half right to left. Burnish. In traditional Japanese style, the folded edges will serve as the fore edges and the open edges will be bound in to the spine.

7. Lay out each page with the folded edge to the right side. Look for interesting spots to place small windows and mark their placement with a pencil and ruler.

8. Open the folded pages, and lay them flat. Use a ruler and craft knife to cut three sides of each window that you marked. Fold open the windows along their uncut side, burnish, and close again.

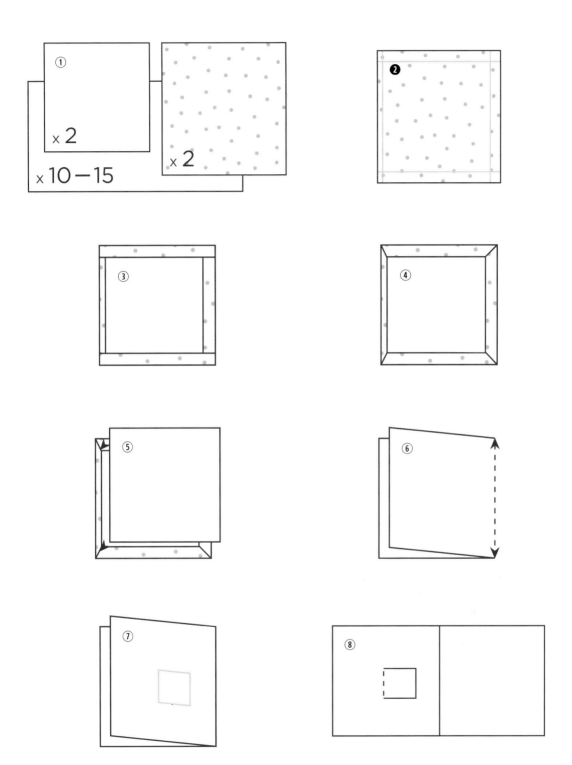

9. Cut out images to go inside the windows. Paste or tape them behind the windows, to the back side of the folded page.

10. Cut a piece of scrap paper to size to serve as a hole punch template. Mark two lines, one ⅜" from the spine edge, and another ³⁄₁₆" from the spine edge. Mark four holes along the inner line, one ⅝" from the top, another ⅝" from the bottom, and the third and fourth evenly distributed between the first two holes. Mark two holes along the outer line, one ⁵⁄₁₆" from the top, and the second ⁵⁄₁₆" from the bottom.

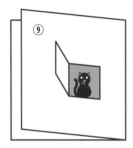

11. Carefully line up the inside pages within the covers and clip them together with a bulldog clip along the fore edge. Place a small scrap of paper between the clip and the covers to prevent the clip from damaging the covers.

12. Use the template to punch holes in the stack of pages along the spine.

13. Stitch the spine following the instructions for the noble binding on pages 80–83.

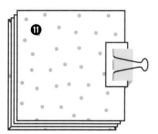
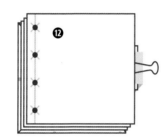
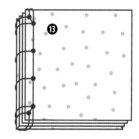

Art Album

See photograph on page 32.

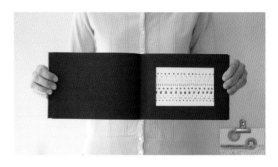

See photograph on page 32.

Finished Size
9½" x 6" x ⅜"

Tools
Metal ruler
Craft knife
Cutting mat or protective surface
Bone folder
Pencil
Paste, glue, or glue stick
Small paste brush (if using paste or glue)
Waxed paper to protect work surface
Book press or heavy stack of books
Bulldog clip
Hole punch (heavy duty for punching through book
    board)
Hammer
Awl
Tapestry needle

Materials
Medium weight paper: 10 to 15 pieces cut to
    18½" x 6"
Template paper: 2 pieces cut to 9¼" x 6"
Book board: 4 pieces, 2 pieces cut to 8⅜" x 6" and
    2 pieces cut to ¾" x 6"
Text weight paper for hinges: 2 pieces cut to 1¾" x 6"
Decorative cover paper: 2 pieces cut to 11⅜" x 8"
Endpaper for inside of covers: 2 pieces cut to
    9¼" x 5⅞"
Title strip: 5" x 1"
Photos or artwork: 10 to 15 pieces, 4" x 6"
Waxed linen thread: 55"

Instructions

1. Trim your papers and book board to size
   with a metal ruler and craft knife.
2. Fold each 18½" x 6" page in half right
   to left. Burnish. In traditional Japanese
   style, the folded edges will serve as the fore
   edges and the open edges will be bound in
   to the spine.
3. Cut a piece of scrap paper to 9¼" x 6"
   to serve as a template for the windows in the
   pages. Draw a line across the template 1¼"
   from the bottom of the page. Draw another
   line across the template 1¼" from the top of
   the page, as well as another line 1¼" from the
   fore edge of the page. Draw a fourth line 2½"
   in from the left edge of the page. The lines
   will form a 5½" x 3½" box in the center of the
   page. Use a metal ruler and craft knife to cut
   out the box.
4. Line up the right edge of the template
   with the folded edge on the right side of a
   page, and mark a box by tracing along the
   window in the template. Repeat until all
   pages are marked.
5. Unfold each page, then use a metal
   ruler and craft knife to cut out the windows along the pencil lines. You will cut
   a window in one side of each unfolded
   page. Refold the pages. When folded,
   the back side of each page will remain
   solid.
6. Draw two vertical lines in the center
   of each piece of hinge paper, leaving a ¼"
   gap between the lines. The ¼" gap will
   serve as a hinge in the cover.

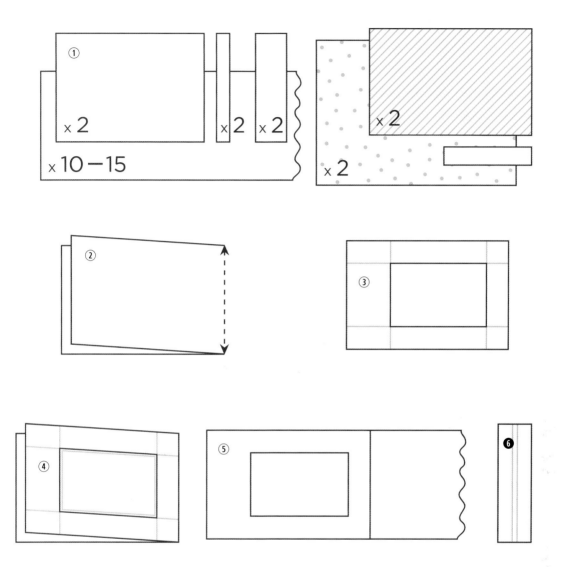

7. Apply a thin layer of paste to the front of a piece of hinge paper. Line up a ¾" piece of book board along the left line of the hinge. Line up an 8⅜" piece of book board along the right line of the hinge. Flip the cover over and smooth. Press until dry. Repeat with the second cover.

8. Lay out the decorative cover papers face down. Draw a line 1" in from each edge to form a box in the center of each paper.

9. Trim all of the corners from the cover papers, leaving ¼" beyond each corner of the penciled in boxes.

10. Apply a thin layer of paste to the back side of one cover paper. Place a hinged cover face down inside of the box that you drew. Flip the hinged cover over onto a piece of waxed paper and smooth to remove air bubbles. Use the bone folder to carefully nudge the cover paper down into the hinge. Be careful to not tear the cover paper at the hinge.

11. Flip again. Fold over the edges, long sides first and short sides last. Smooth.

12. Apply paste to a cover endpaper. Center the paper within the back side of the cover. Smooth. Press.

13. Repeat steps 10 through 12 with the other cover.

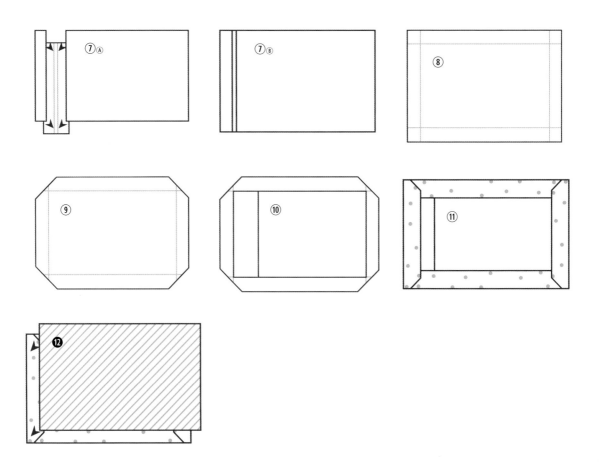

14. Cut a piece of scrap paper to size to serve as a hole punch template. Mark a line ⅜" from the spine edge. Mark four holes along this line, one ⅝" from the top, another ⅝" from the bottom, and the third and fourth evenly distributed between the first two holes.

15. Carefully line up the inside pages and clip with a bulldog clip along the folded ends at the fore edge. Place a small scrap of paper between the clip and the pages to prevent the clip from damaging the pages.

16. Align the template along the spine and punch holes in the pages at the marks.

17. Working with one cover at a time, align the template along the spine and punch holes at the marks with an awl.

18. Stitch the spine following the instructions for the improvised Japanese four-hole binding on page 96–99. To start and finish on the inside is very difficult with a hard cover, so start stitching this project from the outside of the front cover and end up on the outside of the front cover. Tie off on the outside and tie the extra string in a bow. Trim.

19. Adhere the title strip to the center of the front cover.

20. Glue or tape 4" x 6" photos or artwork between the pages, allowing the frame on the front of the page to overlap and frame in the image.

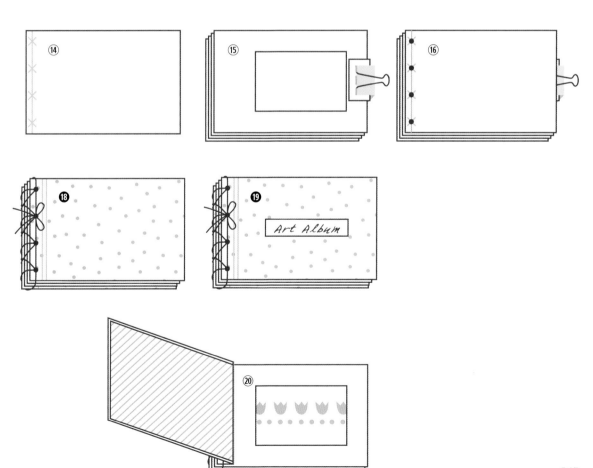

Cut, Keep,
Collage Storage Book

See photograph page 33.

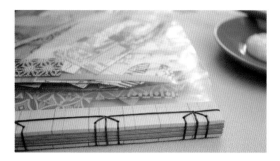

Finished Size
Varies, about 8¾" x 7⅛" x ½"

Tools

Metal ruler
Craft knife
Cutting mat or protective surface
Pencil
Waxed papers
Paste or glue
Medium paste brush
Bone folder
Book press or heavy stack of books
Hole punch (2 mm or ¹⁄₁₆"; Japanese screw punch
    is recommended)
Awl
Tape
2 large safety pins
Tapestry needle

Materials

Plastic freezer bags with zipper seals: 10 bags,
    quart size, about 7⅛" x 8¾"
Chip board: 10 pieces, each ¾" x the width of the
    freezer bags (about 7⅛")
Template paper: Cut to chip board size, ¾" x the
    width of the freezer bags (about 7⅛")
Book board: 2 pieces, cut one piece to ¾" x the
    width of the freezer bags (about 7⅛"), cut
    another piece to the same size as the freezer
    bags (about 8¾" x 7⅛")
Decorative cover paper: 2 pieces, cut one piece to
    the size of the first piece of book board plus 1"
    added to the height and 1" added to the width
    (about 1¾" x 8⅛"), cut another piece to the
    size of the second piece of book board plus 2"
    added to the height and 2" added to the width
    (about 10¾" x 9⅛")
Decorative endpaper: 1 piece to line the back cover,
    cut to the size of the back cover minus ¼"
    from the width and minus ¼" from the height
    (about 8½" x 6⅞")
Waxed linen thread: 1 piece cut to 8x the height of
    the book

Instructions

1. Trim the papers, chip board, and book board to size using a metal ruler and craft knife.
2. Place the decorative cover papers face down. Place a piece of book board in the very center of each paper and trace with a pencil.
3. Trim all corners from the decorative cover papers, leaving ¼" beyond each corner of the penciled in boxes.
4. Apply a thin layer of paste to the back side of the large cover paper. Place the large piece of book board directly inside of the marks. Flip the glued piece over onto waxed paper and smooth the decorative paper to remove air bubbles. Flip again. Fold over the edges, long sides first and short sides last. Smooth.
5. Apply a thin layer of paste to the back side of the decorative endpaper. Center the endpaper within the inside of the back cover. Smooth. Wrap in waxed paper, and press until dry.
6. Repeat step 4 with the small front cover book board and cover paper. Press until dry. There is no need to add an endpaper.

7. Cut a piece of scrap paper to the size of the chip board to serve as a hole punch template. Mark two lines, one ⅜" from the spine edge, and another ³⁄₁₆" from the spine edge. Mark four holes along the inner line, one ⅝" from the top, another ⅝" from the bottom, and the third and fourth evenly distributed between the first two holes. Mark eight holes along the outer line, each one ¼" to either side of the hole marks on the first line.

8. Use the template and hole punch to punch holes into each chip board piece.

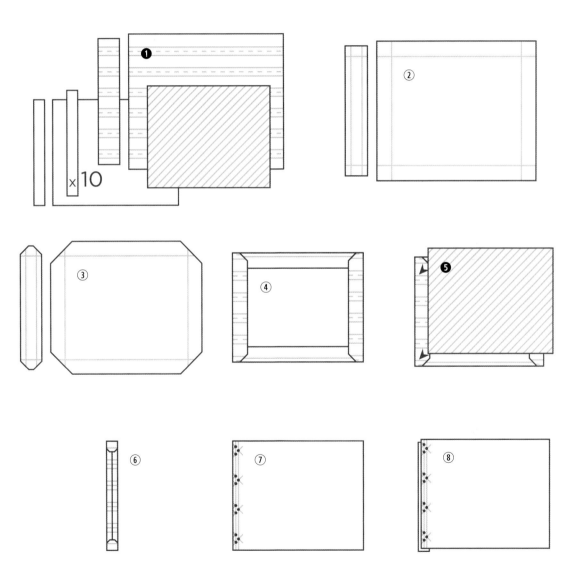

9. Use the template and awl to punch holes into the front and back covers.
10. Punching holes in the bags is tricky because they are slick. Use removable tape to hold one bag at a time down to the cutting mat. Line up the hole punch template along the end of the bag (the end opposite of the zipper) and tape it down as well. Punch. Repeat with all bags.

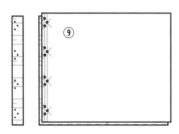

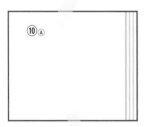

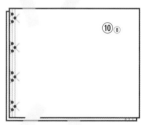

11. Use two large safety pins to line up the pages and hold them in place for stitching. Open up the pins and secure the materials through the top and bottom holes: back cover (facing down), chip board, zipper bag (alternate the rest of the chip boards and zipper bags), and front cover strip (facing up).

12. Stitch the spine following the instructions for the tortoise-shell binding on pages 90–95.

    Here are a few tips specifically for this project:

    - Start from the inside, right between the first bag and the chip board below it.

    - Remove each safety pin when you get to it during the stitching process.

    - The last step is tricky. Instead of proceeding through hole 2 from the back to the inside of the book, bring your needle all the way through hole 2 from back to front. Approach the inside of the book from the front. Be careful to not break your needle when going back inside the front cover. If you cannot get your needle back inside the front cover to tie off, pull the inside thread out of the front cover and tie it off on the outside of the front cover. Tie the threads in a bow.

13. Write on the bag labels with a permanent pen or adhere a label to each bag to note its contents.

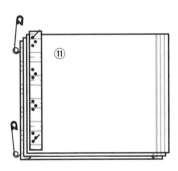

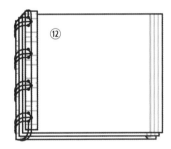

My Favorite Recipes

See photograph on pages 34–35.

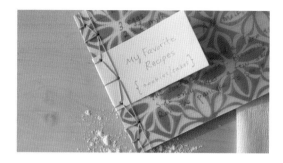

Instructions

1. Trim the covers and label to size with a metal ruler and craft knife.

2. Use an extra index card to serve as a hole punch template. Mark two lines, one ⅜" from the spine edge and another 3⁄16" from the spine edge. Mark three holes along the inner line, one ¾" from the top, another ¾" from the bottom, and the third in the very center. Mark four holes along the outer line, each one evenly distributed between the hole marks on the first line.

3. Use the template to punch holes in each cover and in the pages. For the plastic covers, you may find a small hole punch easier to use than an awl.

4. Score the label ½" from the left edge and fold it under to the back.

5. Wrap the folded end of the label around the spine side of the front cover. Center the label from top to bottom. Use the template to mark the punch holes on the label. Remove label from front cover and punch holes at the marks through both layers of the folded edge.

6. Hold the punched label in place around the spine of the front cover. Align the pages between both covers. Clip with a bulldog clip along the fore edge. Place a small scrap of paper between the clip and the covers to prevent the clip from damaging the covers.

7. Stitch the spine following the instructions for the hemp-leaf binding on pages 84–89. This project adapts the hemp-leaf binding from nine to seven holes. As you follow the stitching instructions omit holes 3 and 3a. Continue to follow the same stitching pattern shown.

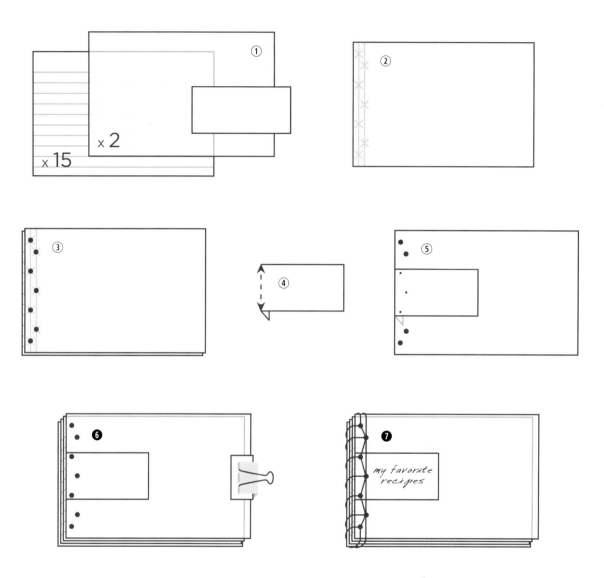

My Favorite Cleaning Recipes

See photograph on pages 36–37.

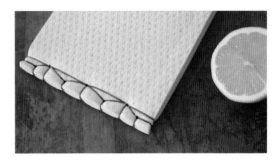

Finished Size

6⅛" x 4⅛" x ½"

Tools

Metal ruler
Craft knife
Cutting mat or protective cutting surface
Pencil
Awl or small hole punch
Bone folder
Bulldog clip
Needle
Scissors

Materials

Index cards: 15 cards, each 6" x 4"
Thin sponge cloth (about ³⁄₁₆" thick): 2 pieces, cut
  to 6⅛" x 4⅛"
Extra index card for template: 6" x 4"
Waxed linen thread: 40"

Instructions

1. Allow new sponges to air dry for 24 hours, as they will shrink. The sponges should be flexible enough to fold once dry. If your sponge is not flexible, you may need to try a different brand.
2. Trim your covers to size with a metal ruler and sharp craft knife.
3. Use an extra index card to serve as a hole punch template. Mark two lines, one ⅜" from the spine edge and another ³⁄₁₆" from the spine edge. Mark three holes along the inner line, one ¾" from the top, another ¾" from the bottom, and the third in the very center. Mark four holes along the outer line, each one evenly distributed between the hole marks on the first line.
4. Use the template to punch holes in each cover and in the pages.
5. Align the pages between both covers. Clip with a bulldog clip along the fore edge. Place a small scrap of paper between the clip and the covers to prevent the clip from damaging the covers.
6. Stitch the spine following the instructions for the hemp-leaf binding on pages 84–89. This project adapts the hemp-leaf binding from nine to seven holes. As you follow the stitching instructions omit holes 3 and 3a. Continue to follow the same stitching pattern shown.

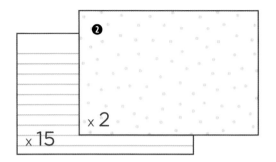

❷

x 2

x 15

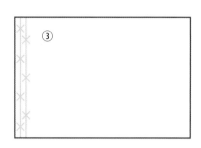

③

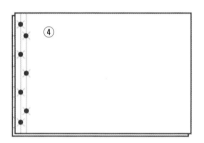

④

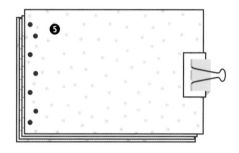

❺

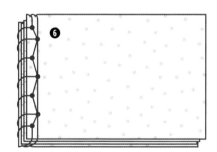

❻

P.S. Letter Collection

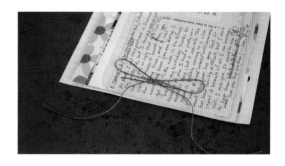

See photograph on page 40.

Finished Size
Varies

Tools

Cutting mat or protective cutting surface
Pencil
Bulldog clip
Awl
Needle

Materials

Selection of cards, notes, letters, and envelopes:
    Up to 20 items
Thread: 20"

Instructions

1. Line up your selection of papers along one end. Keep in mind that the bound edge will conceal writing and images. Rotate or flip your items to make the most important information visible.

2. Clip the pages together with a bulldog clip at a location where all pages overlap. Place a small scrap of paper between the clip and the pages to prevent the clip from damaging the pages. Mark two holes at ½" from the spine, with 2" between them. These holes should go through all of the pages.

3. Use an awl to punch holes at the marks all the way through the stack of papers.

4. Stitch the spine following the instructions for the Yamato binding on pages 100–101.

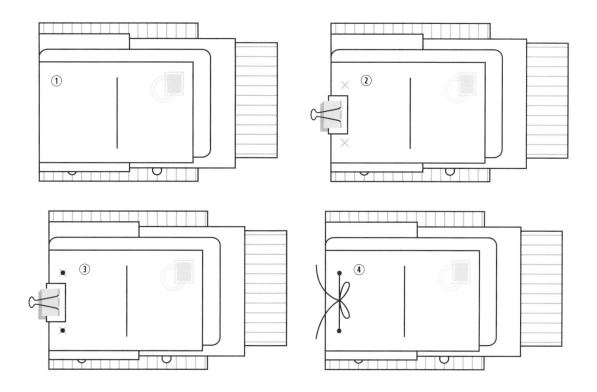

Leaflet Memo Pad

See photograph on page 41.

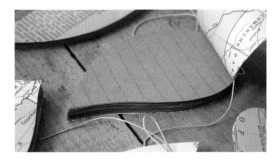

Finished Size
Varies

Tools

Metal ruler
Craft knife or scissors
Cutting mat or protective cutting surface
Pencil
Eraser
Bulldog clip
Awl
Needle

Materials

Decorative paper for cover: 2 pieces, each 4" x 5"
Text weight paper: 30 pieces, each 4" x 5"
Template paper: 4" x 5"
String (10 lb. jewelry hemp cord): 14"

Instructions

1. Trim the covers and pages to size with a metal ruler and craft knife.
2. Create a leaf-shaped template within the 4" x 5" page by tracing a real leaf, drawing your own, or using the template on pages 161. Cut out the template.
3. Use a pencil to trace the template onto each inside page.
4. Cut out each page along the pencil line with scissors or a craft knife. Expect each page to vary just a bit in size once they are cut out.
5. Use a pencil to trace the template onto each cover paper. Draw the line a bit larger than the template, about $1/16$" to $1/8$" larger. Remember to turn the template over to trace it onto the back cover. Cut out each cover.
6. Carefully center the stack of inside pages within the two covers and clip them together with a bulldog clip at the fore edge. Place a small scrap of paper between the clip and the covers to prevent the clip from damaging the covers.

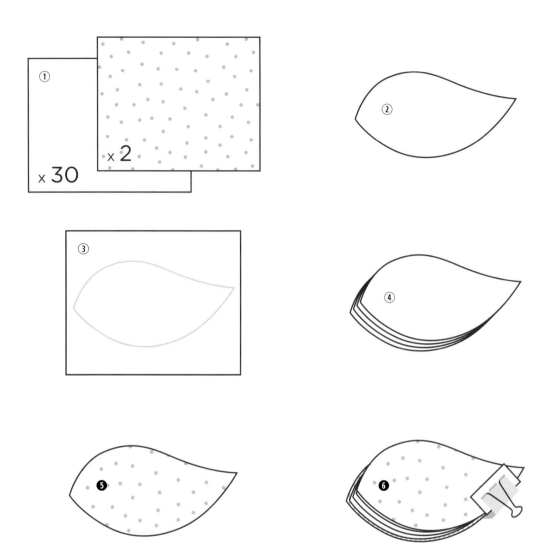

① x 30

x 2

②

③

④

⑤

⑥

7. Mark two holes at the spine, at least ⅛" from any edge. Mark the holes about ½" to ¾" apart from each other.

8. Punch through the entire thickness with an awl.

9. Stitch the spine following the instructions for the Yamato binding on pages 100–101.

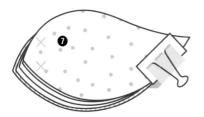

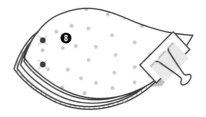

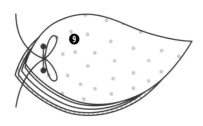

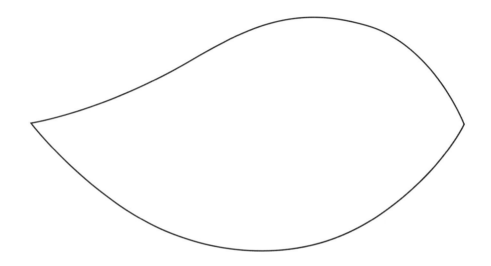

Actual size template

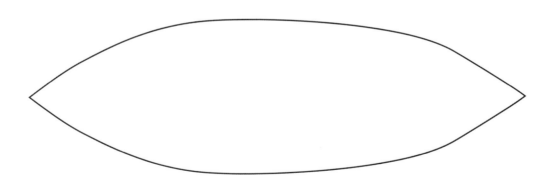

Actual size template

Sock Book

See photograph on pages 42–43.

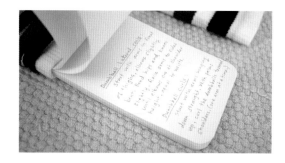

Finished Size

Varies, about 7¼" x 3¼" x ⅜"

Tools

Metal ruler
Craft knife or scissors
Cutting mat or protective cutting
    surface
Corner rounder or scissors
Bulldog clip
Waxed paper
Small glue brush
PVA or white glue
Pencil
Awl
Fabric scissors
Sewing needle and thread

Materials

Tube or crew sock
Heavy weight paper (80 lb. drawing paper):
    30 pieces (see step 1 to determine size)
Template paper: Cut to inside page size
Embroidery floss: 14"

Instructions

1. Measure the top portion of the sock. With the sock lying flat, measure the length from the line where the weave meets the foot of the sock to the top. Your inside pages will be ¼" shorter than the sock width and ½" shorter than the sock length (i.e., if the sock is 3¼" x 7½", the pages will be 3" x 7").

2. Trim your papers to size with a metal ruler and craft knife.

3. Round the fore edge corners of each page. This will help keep the pages from snagging on the sock.

4. Align the inside pages and clip them with a bulldog clip along the fore edge. Place a small scrap of paper between the clip and the pages to prevent the clip from damaging the pages.

5. Lay the book block flat on a piece of waxed paper. Slide the spine of the book just off of the edge of your work surface. Brush on a thin layer of glue along the spine. Let the glue dry completely.

6. Cut a piece of scrap paper to the inside page size to serve as a hole punch template. Mark a line ½" from the spine edge. Mark two holes along this line, evenly distributed between the edges of the page.

7. Use the template to punch holes through the pages at the spine.

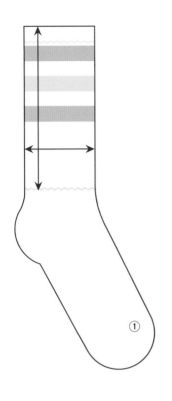

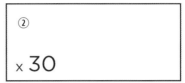

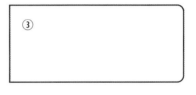

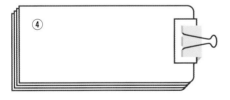

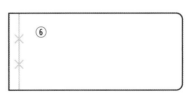

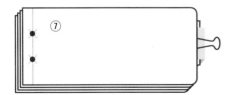

8. Cut the foot off of the sock, ½" past the end of the weave.
9. Turn the tube of the sock wrong side out.
10. Thread a sewing needle with thread that matches the color of the sock. Tie a knot in the end of the thread. Hand sew the end of the sock tube closed along the edge of the weave (½" in from the cut edge). Tie off the end of the thread and trim any excess thread.
11. Trim off some of the extra fabric, leaving ⅛" to ¼" of fabric past the hand sewing. Turn the sock right side out.

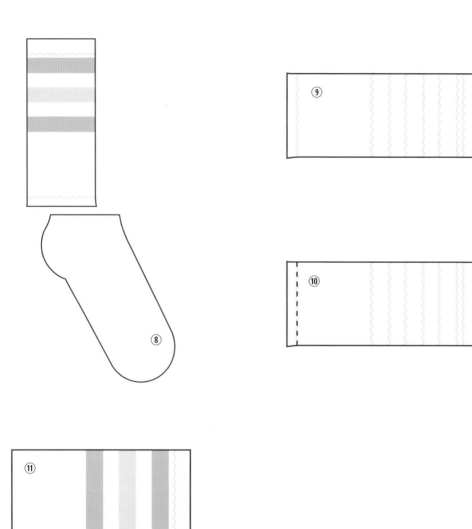

12. Remove the bulldog clip from the inside pages and slide them into the cover. Line the spine of the pages up against the hand-sewn seam.

13. Stitch the spine following the instructions for the Yamato binding on pages 100–101. Stitch directly through the sock, without punching holes. Because you cannot see the binding holes from the outside, you may need to poke around for the holes until the end of your needle finds them.

14. Open the front cover by scrunching the sock back toward the spine.

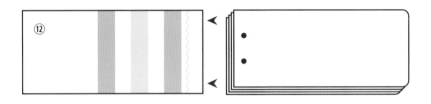

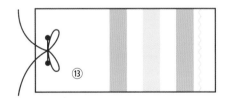

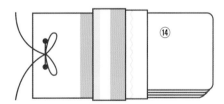

Pillowcase Dream Journal

See photograph on pages 44–45.

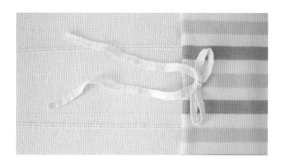

Finished Size
8½" x 7" x ⅜"

Tools
Metal ruler
Craft knife
Cutting mat or protective cutting surface
Corner rounder or scissors
Bulldog clip
Waxed paper
Small glue brush
Glue
Pencil
Awl
Fabric scissors
Ironing board
Iron
Fabric pins
Sewing machine
Sewing thread to match pillowcase fabric
Cotton swab
Needle

Materials
Woven fabric for pillowcase: Cut to 7" x 14½"
Woven fabric for trim: Cut to 5½" x 14½"
Heavy weight paper (80 lb. drawing paper):
    30 pieces, each 5½" x 7"
Template paper: Cut to inside page size 5½" x 7"
Ribbon or embroidery floss: 24"

Instructions:

1. Trim your papers to size with a metal ruler and craft knife.

2. Round the fore edge corners of each page. This will help keep the pages from snagging on the fabric cover.

3. Align the pages and clip them with a bulldog clip along the fore edge. Place a small scrap of paper between the clip and the pages to prevent the clip from damaging the pages.

4. Lay the book block flat on a piece of waxed paper. Slide the spine of the book just off of the edge of your work surface. Brush on a thin layer of glue along the spine. Let the glue dry completely.

5. Cut a piece of scrap paper to the inside page size to serve as a hole punch template. Mark a line ½" from the spine edge. Mark two holes along this line, evenly distributed between the top and bottom edges of the page.

6. Use the template to punch holes through the pages at the spine. Use an awl if you plan to bind the cover with thin thread or a hole punch if you plan to use ribbon.

7. Cut the fabric pieces to size.

8. Lay the trim fabric right side down onto your ironing board. Fold each of the long edges ½" to the wrong side and press it with a hot iron.

9. Fold the trim fabric in half lengthwise, right side out, and press it with a hot iron.

10. Lay the pillowcase fabric flat onto your work surface. Sandwich one long edge within the folded trim fabric, overlapping ½". Pin it in place.

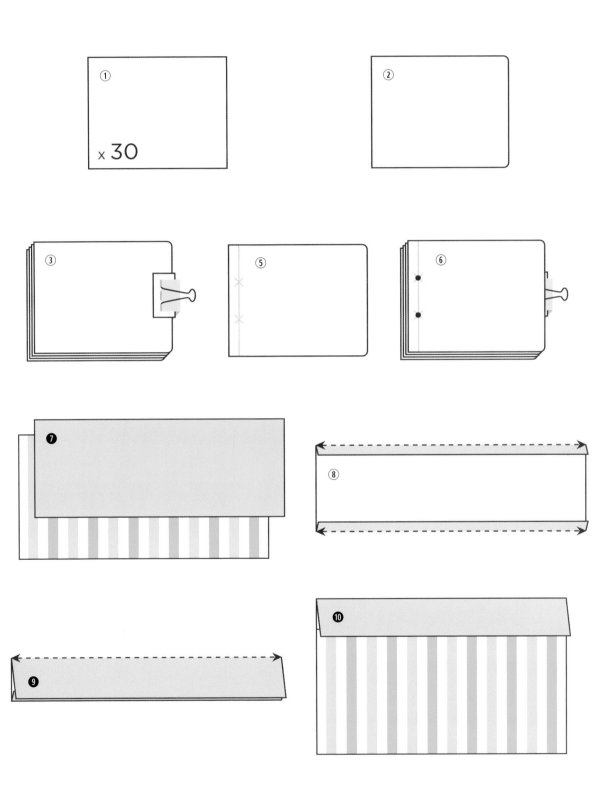

11. Using a sewing machine, top stitch along the pinned edge, ⅛" in from the folded edge of the trim. Remove the pins as you sew.

12. Fold the pillowcase in half, wrong side facing out. Pin along the two unfinished edges. Using a sewing machine, stitch ¼" in along the pinned edges, removing the pins as you sew. Zigzag stitch along the raw edges to prevent fraying.

13. Turn the pillowcase right side out and press it with a hot iron.

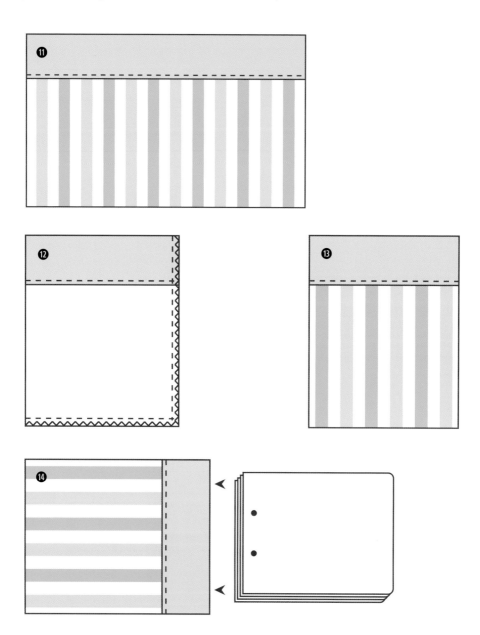

14. With the sewn edges at the bottom and left side, slide the inside pages into the cover. Line the spine of the pages up against the seam, centered from top to bottom. Clip along the spine with a bulldog clip. If using thread that can penetrate fabric with a needle, skip to step 19.

15. If using a ribbon or thicker thread that cannot go through fabric with just a needle, use a pencil to mark two holes in the fabric cover. Align the marks with the holes of the inside pages.

16. Remove the clip and pages and lay the pillowcase flat on a cutting mat. Punch holes at the marks with a very sharp hole punch or snip a tiny hole with scissors.

17. Place a piece of waxed paper inside of the pillowcase. To prevent fraying, use a cotton swab to apply a tiny bit of glue to all four holes (two in the front of the cover and two in the back of the cover). Let dry completely. Remove waxed paper.

18. Slide the pages back into the pillowcase and clip. Place a small scrap of paper between the clip and the pillowcase to prevent the clip from damaging the pillowcase.

19. Stitch the spine following the instructions for the Yamato binding on pages 100–101. If you cannot see the binding holes from the outside, you may need to poke for the holes until the end of your needle finds them. To stitch the spine with ribbon, wrap a tiny piece of paper around the end to assist it through the holes.

20. Open the front cover by scrunching the pillowcase back toward the spine.

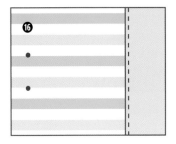

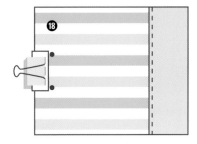

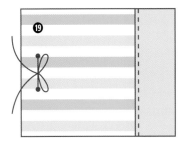

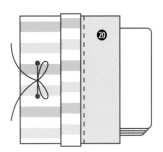

Sweet Secrets Sachet Book

See photograph on pages 46–47.

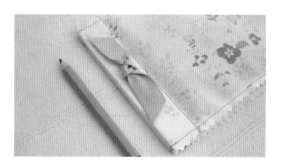

Instructions:

1. Trim your papers to size with a metal ruler
   and craft knife. Make sure that the grain of
   the papers and chip board runs parallel to
   their height.
2. Fold each text weight page in half
   right to left. Burnish. In the traditional
   Japanese style, the folded edges will serve
   as the fore edges and the open edges will
   be bound in to the spine.
3. Align the pages and clip at the fore
   edge (folded edges) with a bulldog clip.
   Place a small scrap of paper between the
   clip and the pages to prevent the clip from
   damaging the pages.
4. Cut a piece of scrap paper to the
   inside page size to serve as a hole punch
   template. Mark a line ½" from the spine
   edge. Mark two holes along this line, evenly
   distributed between the edges of the page.
5. Use the template to punch holes through
   the pages at the spine. Create a hole that will
   accommodate the thickness of the ribbon.
6. Trim the fabric to size.
7. Fold each piece of fabric in half left to
   right with the right side out. Press with a hot
   iron.
8. Using a sewing machine, stitch along
   the folded edge of the top cover piece, ¾"
   in from the fold. This pocket will hold a
   piece of chip board.
9. Slide the small, ¾" x 4" piece of chip
   board into the pocket you just created.
   Center from top to bottom.
10. Pin one 10" piece of ribbon to the top
    cover piece at the center of the fore edge,
    between the layers of fabric. Place the end of
    the ribbon 1" in from the edge of the fabric.

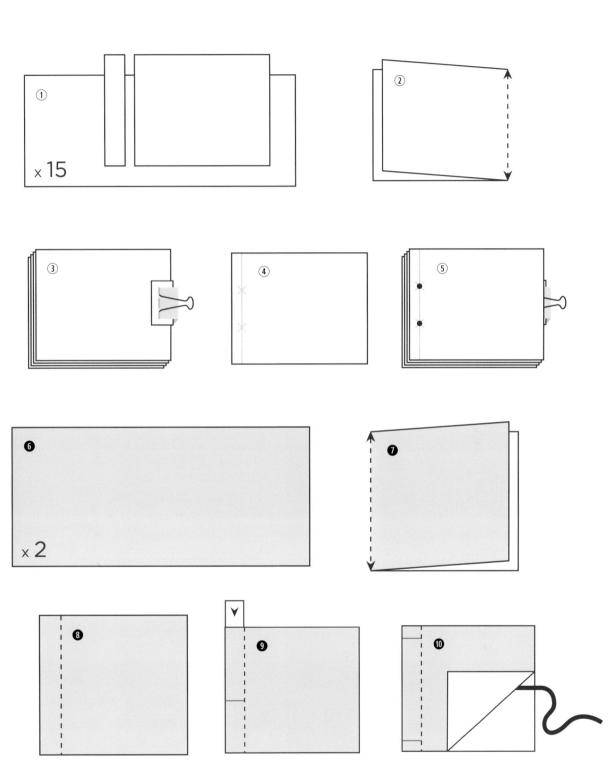

11. With the small chip board piece and ribbon pinned in place, machine stitch along the top edge of the front cover, with a ½" seam allowance. Stop and turn at the corner, continuing to sew along the fore edge with a ½" seam allowance, stopping to backstitch at the ribbon for reinforcement and removing the pin. Stop and turn at the corner. Continue to sew along the bottom edge. Stop when halfway across the bottom edge.

12. Pour ¼ cup of dried lavender into the front cover through the hole left along the bottom edge. Roll a piece of scrap paper into a funnel to assist you.

13. Resume machine stitching along the bottom edge. Backstitch when you get to the edge of the spine.

14. For the back cover, fold the back fabric in half, right side out, and pin one 10" piece of ribbon at the center of the fore edge, between the layers of fabric. Place the end of the ribbon 1" in from the edge of the fabric.

15. With the ribbon pinned in place, machine stitch along the top edge of the back cover, with a ½" seam allowance.

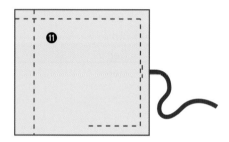

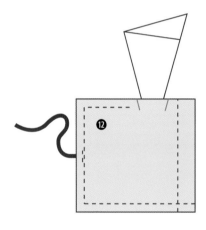

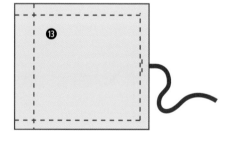

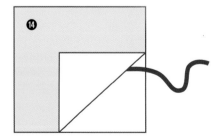

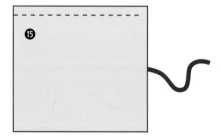

16. Slide the 5" x 4" chip board piece between the layers of fabric, snug against the fold and sewn edge.
17. Hold the chip board in place as you continue to sew around the perimeter of the back cover, stopping to backstitch at the ribbon for reinforcement. Trim the threads.
18. Use a pair of pinking shears to trim the excess fabric along all sewn edges of both covers, leave about ¼" of fabric past the stitching. Be careful when you get to the ribbons!
19. Use the hole punch template to punch holes through each cover at the spine.
20. Place a piece of waxed paper over your work surface. To prevent fraying, use a cotton swab to apply a tiny bit of glue to all four holes. Let the glue dry completely.
21. With a bulldog clip securing the fore edges of the inside pages, carefully center them within the two covers. You may not be able to clip the covers to the pages due to the nature of the materials. Gently hold the covers in place while stitching. Stitch the spine following the instructions for the Yamato binding on pages 100–101. To thread the ribbon, wrap a tiny piece of paper around the end to assist it through the holes.
22. Tie the two ribbons at the fore edge in a bow.

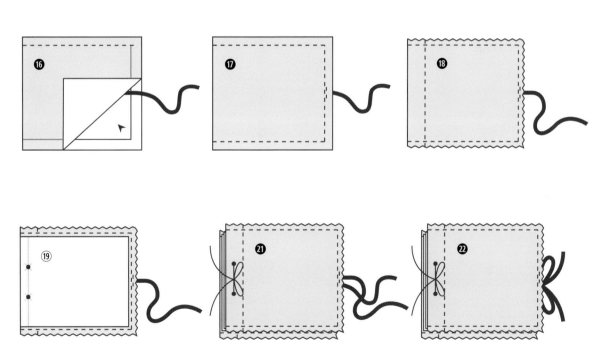

Sewing Notions
Pincushion Book

See photograph on pages 48–49.

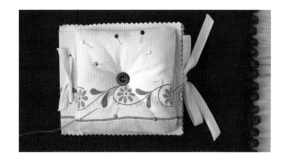

Instructions

1. Trim your papers to size with a metal ruler and craft knife. Make sure that the grain of the papers and chip board is parallel to the height.

2. Fold each text weight page in half right to left. Burnish. In the traditional Japanese style, the folded edges will serve as the fore edges and the open edges will be bound in to the spine.

3. Align the pages and clip them at the fore edge (folded edges) with a bulldog clip. Place a small scrap of paper between the clip and the pages to prevent the clip from damaging the pages.

4. Cut a piece of scrap paper to the inside page size to serve as a hole punch template. Mark a line ½" from the spine edge. Mark two holes along this line, evenly distributed between the edges of the page.

5. Use the template to punch holes through the pages at the spine. Create a hole that will accommodate the thickness of the ribbon.

6. Trim the fabric to size.

7. Fold each 11" x 5" piece of fabric in half, right side out. Press with a hot iron.

8. Using a sewing machine, stitch along the folded edge of the top cover piece, ¾" in from the fold. This pocket will hold a piece of chip board.

9. Slide the small ¾" x 4" piece of chip board into the pocket you just created. Center from top to bottom.

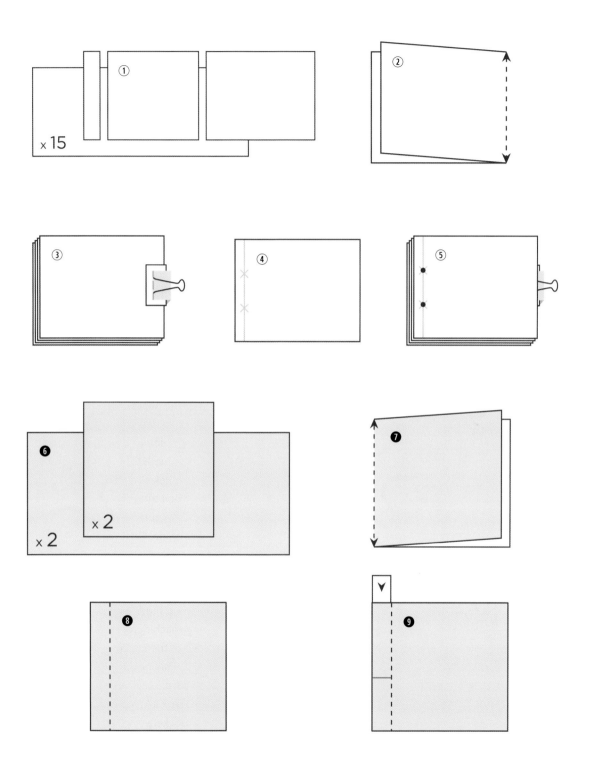

10. Pin one 10" piece of ribbon at the center of the fore edge, between the layers of fabric. Place the end of the ribbon 1" in from the edge of the fabric.

11. With the small chip board piece and ribbon pinned in place, machine stitch along the top edge of the front cover, with a ½" seam allowance. Stop at the corner.

12. Slide the 4⅛" x 4" chip board piece between the layers of fabric, snug against the two sewn edges.

13. Hold the chip board in place as you continue to sew around the perimeter of the front cover, stopping to backstitch at the ribbon for reinforcement. Backstitch when you get to the edge of the spine.

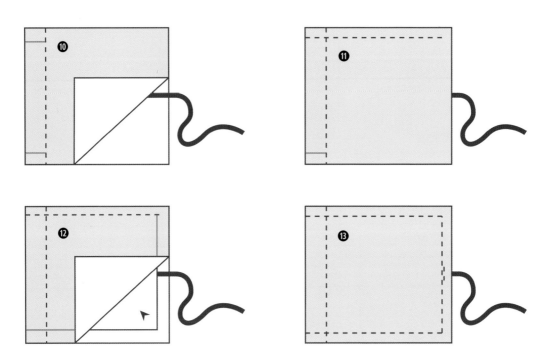

14. For the back cover, pin one 10" piece of ribbon at the center of the fore edge, between the layers of fabric. Place the end of the ribbon 1" in from the edge of the fabric.
15. With the ribbon pinned in place, machine stitch along the top edge of the back cover, with a ½" seam allowance.
16. Slide the 5" x 4" chip board piece between the layers of fabric, snug against the fold and sewn edge.

17. Hold the chip board in place as you continue to sew around the perimeter of the back cover, stopping to backstitch at the ribbon for reinforcement. Trim the threads.
18. Use a pair of pinking shears to trim the excess fabric along all sewn edges of both covers, leave about ¼" of fabric past the stitching. Be careful when you get to the ribbons!

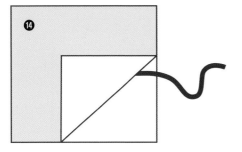

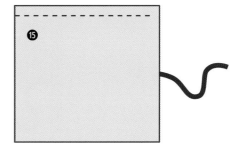

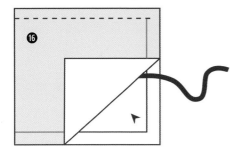

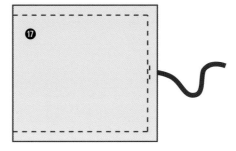

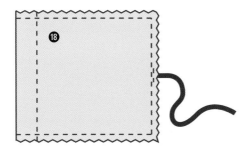

19. Center the hole punch template along the spine to punch holes through each cover.
20. Place a piece of waxed paper over your work surface. To prevent fraying, use a cotton swab to apply a tiny bit of glue to the fabric at all four holes. Let the glue dry completely.
21. Pin the two 5½" x 5½" pieces of fabric right sides together.
22. Machine stitch around the edges with a ½" seam allowance, leaving a 2" hole in one side.
23. Turn the pillow right side out through the 2" hole. Fill the pillow with polyester fiberfill until lightly firm. Hand sew the hole closed.
24. Hand sew each corner of the pillow down to the corners of the right side of the front cover panel.

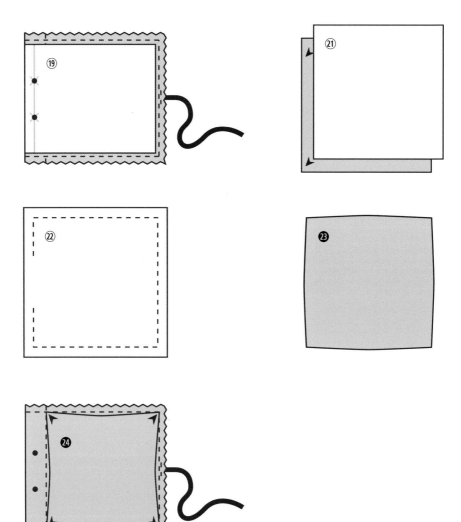

25. Place the front cover on a protective cutting mat. Center one button on top of the pillow and press it down toward the mat. At each hole in the button, poke an awl all the way through the pillow and chip board to the mat.

26. Place the other button opposite the first button on the inside of the front cover.

27. Hand sew both of the buttons to the front cover at once, using double thread and pulling firmly. Go up through the bottom button, through the cover and pillow, up through the top button, and loop back down. Repeat several times and tie off the thread at the bottom button. Wrap the thread around the bottom button four times and trim.

28. With a bulldog clip securing the fore edges of the inside pages carefully center them within the two covers. You may not be able to clip the covers to the pages due to the nature of the materials. Gently hold the covers in place while stitching. Stitch the spine following the instructions for the Yamato binding on pages 100–101. To thread through the ribbon, wrap a tiny piece of paper around the end to assist it through the holes.

29. Tie the two ribbons at the fore edge in a bow.

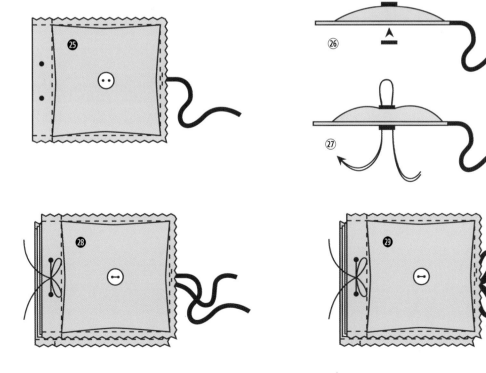

Tea Bag Tracing Book

See photograph on page 52.

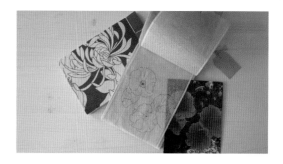

Finished Size
Varies, about 5⅞" x 3⅞"

Tools
Iron
Ironing board
Metal ruler
Craft knife
Cutting mat or protective cutting surface
Hole punch
Pencil
Bulldog clip
Awl
Needle

Materials
Tea bags: 50 pages
Thread (silk thread or waxed linen thread): 2
    threads, each 5x the book's width
Cover stock paper (thick paper or tea box): 2 cov-
    ers, each to match the size of the tea bags,
    about 5⅞" x 3⅞"
Template paper: Cut to cover size
Cover stock paper for tag: 1" x 1½"

Instructions:

1. Collect the tea bags over time. After making tea, allow the bag to cool. While still moist, remove the staple and/or string. Discard the tea leaves and rinse the bag. Lay the bag flat to dry.
2. Prepare tea bags by ironing them on an ironing board on a low heat setting.
3. Trim the papers to size with a metal ruler and craft knife.
4. Trim the two corners on the top of the tag paper. Punch a small hole at the top, centered between the trimmed corners.
5. Cut a piece of scrap paper to the cover size to serve as a hole punch template. Mark a line ½" from the spine edge. Mark two holes along this line, evenly distributed between the edges of the page.
6. Carefully line up the tea bags between the covers and clip with a bulldog clip along the fore edge. Place a small scrap of paper between the clip and the covers to prevent the clip from damaging the covers.
7. Use the template to punch holes through the covers and pages at the spine.
8. Stitch the spine following the instructions for the account book binding on pages 102–3.
9. Thread all four threads through the tag and tie off. Fray the threads and trim them.
10. Use the delicate pages as you would use tracing paper to trace photos and other images.

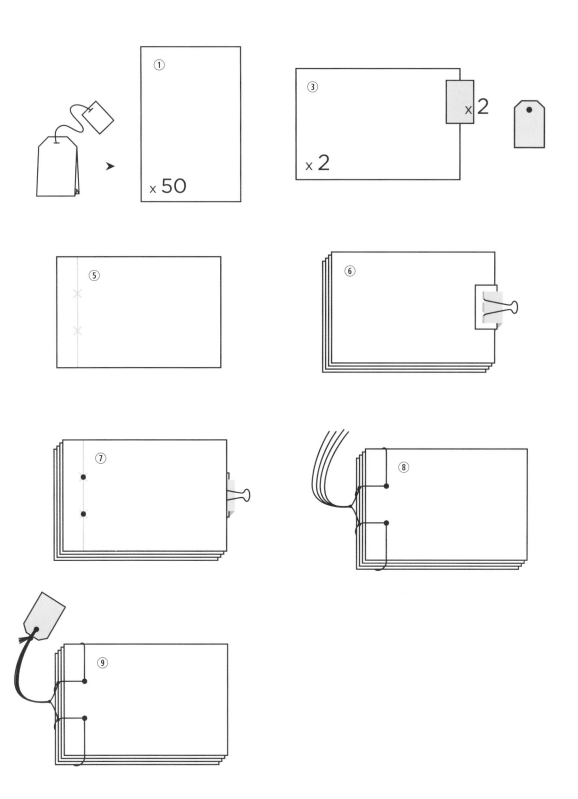

① x 50

③ x 2   x 2

⑤

⑥

⑦

⑧

⑨

Gardener's Journal

See photograph on page 53.

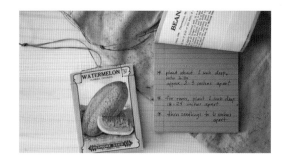

Finished Size
Varies

Tools

Metal ruler
Craft knife
Cutting mat or protective cutting surface
Pencil
Bulldog clip
Awl
Needle

Materials

Seed packet: 1 packet
Text weight paper: 30 pages, cut to cover size
Chip board: 1 piece, cut to cover size
Template paper: Cut to cover size
String (10 lb. jewelry hemp cord): 2 threads, each
   5x the book's width

Instructions

1. Measure the dimensions of your seed packet.
2. Trim your papers to the size of your seed packet with a metal ruler and craft knife.
3. Cut a piece of scrap paper to the cover size to serve as a hole punch template. Mark a line ½" from the spine edge. Mark two holes along this line, evenly distributed between the edges of the page. You can adjust the location of the holes to accommodate the design on the front cover, if necessary.
4. Arrange your papers in order: chip board on bottom, pages in the middle, and the seed packet facing up on the top. Clip with a bulldog clip along the fore edge. Place a small scrap of paper between the clip and the pages to prevent the clip from damaging the pages.
5. Use the template to punch holes through the covers and pages at the spine.
6. Stitch the spine following the instructions for the account book binding on pages 102–3.
7. Knot the ends of the strings together to create a loop for hanging the book in a tool shed or on a potting bench.

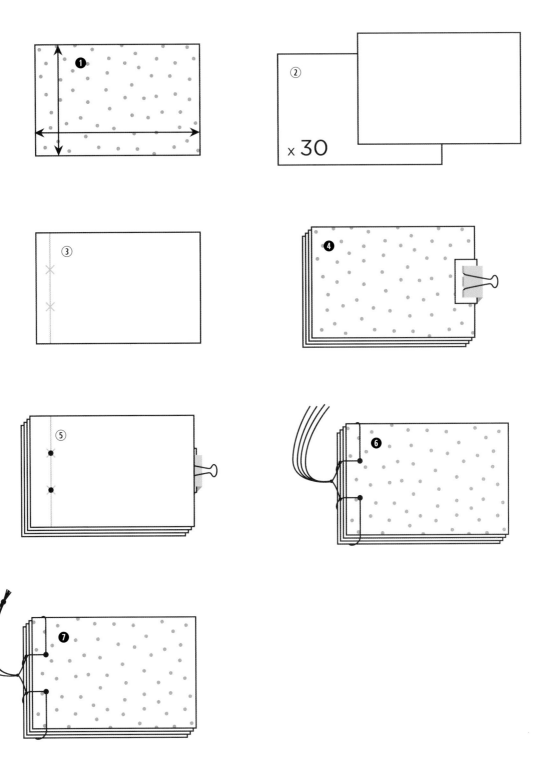

Wall Art Drawing Pad

See photographs on pages 54–55.

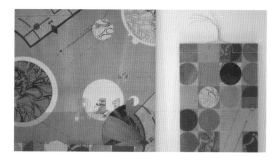

Finished Size

Varies

Tools

Metal ruler
Craft knife
Cutting mat or protective cutting surface
Bulldog clips
Waxed paper
Small glue brush
Glue
Pencil
Awl
Needle

Materials

Cover paper (poster, calendar image, etc.): 1 piece
Drawing paper: 30 pages, cut to cover size
Chip board: 1 piece, cut to cover size
Template paper: Cut to cover size
String (10 lb. jewelry hemp cord): 2 threads, each
    5x the book's width (if book is wider than 6",
    you will need 4 threads, each 2x the book's
    width)

Instructions

1. Measure the dimensions of the cover.
2. Trim the papers and chip board to
   the size of the cover with a metal ruler and
   craft knife.
3. Arrange the papers in order: chip board
   on bottom, pages in the middle, and the
   cover facing up on the top. Clip with bulldog
   clips along the fore edge, as well as on both
   sides near the spine. Place a small scrap of
   paper between each clip and the covers to
   prevent the clips from damaging the covers.
4. Lay the book block flat on a piece of
   waxed paper. Slide the spine of the book
   just off of the edge of your work surface.
   Brush on a thin layer of glue along the
   spine. Let dry completely. Remove clips
   near spine.
5. Cut a piece of scrap paper to the
   cover size to serve as a hole punch template. Mark a line ½" from the spine edge.
   Mark two holes along this line, evenly
   distributed between the edges of the
   page.

   If the book is more than 6" wide, make
   four additional marks, two evenly spaced
   above the top hole and two evenly spaced
   below the bottom hole. You will mark a
   total of six holes.
6. Use the template to punch holes
   through the covers and pages at the spine.
7. Stitch the spine following the instructions for the account book binding on
   pages 102–3.

   If the book is more than 6" wide and you
   created six holes, follow the instructions for
   the account book binding twice, following
   the instructions to separately bind each set
   of three holes.
8. Knot the ends of the strings together
   to create a loop for hanging.

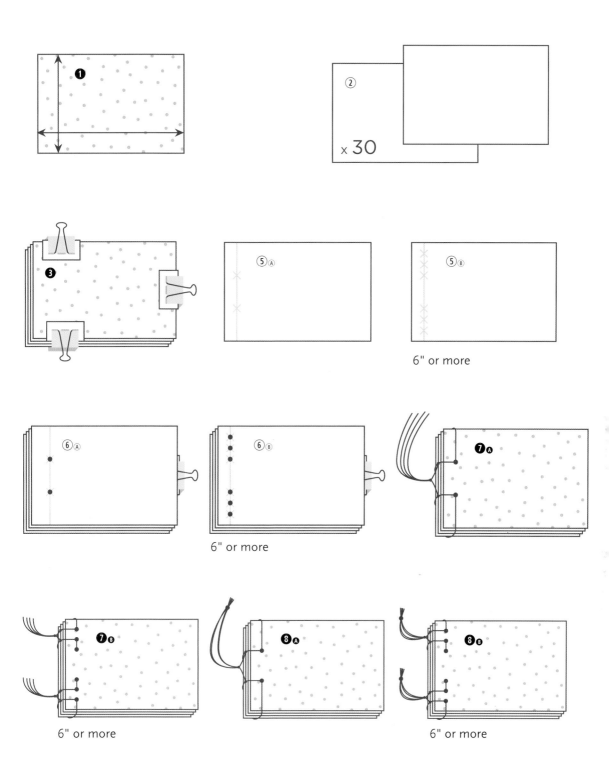

6" or more

6" or more

6" or more

6" or more

Gift Tag Book

See photograph on page 58.

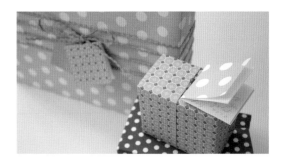

Finished Size

2" square

Tools

Metal ruler
Craft knife
Cutting mat or protective cutting surface
Bone folder
Pencil
Awl or small hole punch
Needle
Scissors

Materials

Wrapping paper: 1 piece, cut to 2" x 4"
Text weight paper: 1 or 2 pieces, each cut to
    3⅞" x 1⁵⁄₁₆"
Template paper: Cut to inside page size, 3⅞" x 1⁵⁄₁₆"
String or embroidery floss: 12"
Small bead

Instructions

1. Trim the papers to size with a metal ruler and craft knife.
2. Fold each paper in half left to right, including the template paper and the cover paper. Burnish.
3. Open the template paper and use the pencil to mark three holes along the inside fold. Make one mark directly in the center, and the other two marks ½" out each way from the center.
4. Nest the template within the pages and cover, centering the pages directly within the cover. Lay the book down on the cutting mat, cover facing down. Punch holes at the marks through all layers.
5. Sew the spine following the instructions for the ledger binding on pages 104–5.
6. After tying off, thread on a small bead. Tie another double knot to secure the bead.
7. Attach the completed book to a gift or wrapped package.

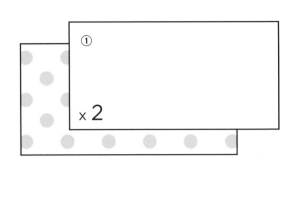

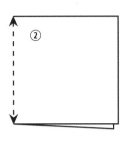

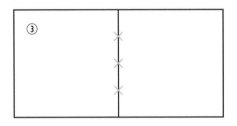

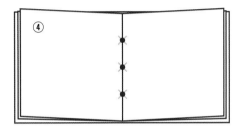

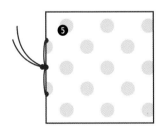

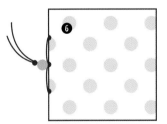

Recycle Bin Memo Pad

See photograph on page 59.

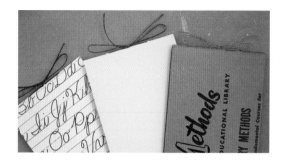

Finished Size
3" x 5⅞" x ⅛"

Tools
Metal ruler
Craft knife
Cutting mat or protective cutting surface
Bone folder
Pencil
Awl or small hole punch
Needle
Scissors
Book press or heavy stack of books

Materials
Cover stock paper: 1 piece, cut to 3" x 11¾"
Text weight paper: 10 pieces, cut to 2⅝" x 11"
Template paper: Cut to inside page size,
    2⅝" x 11"
String, thread, or ribbon: 12"

Instructions

1. Trim the papers to size with a metal ruler and craft knife.
2. Fold each paper in half left to right, including the template paper and the cover paper. Burnish.
3. Open the template paper and use the pencil to mark three holes along the inside fold. Mark one hole directly in the center. Mark each of the other two holes halfway between the center hole and the edge of the page.
4. Nest the template within the pages and cover, centering the pages directly within the cover. Lay the book down on the cutting mat, cover facing down. Punch holes at the marks through all layers.
5. Sew the spine following the instructions for the ledger binding on pages 104–5.
6. After tying off, tie the extra thread in a small bow. Trim any excess thread.
7. If necessary, press the completed book to flatten the spine.

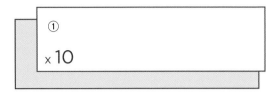

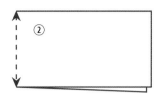

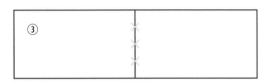

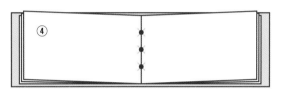

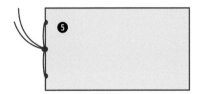

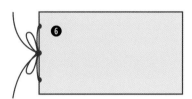

RES●URCES

You will find many basic tools and supplies at your local arts and crafts store, office supply store, and hardware store. To find particular bookbinding tools and supplies, take a look at some of these online sources.

BLICK ART MATERIALS
www.dickblick.com

A great resource for all art materials, Blick carries basic bookbinding tools and other art tools that work well for bookbinding.

HIROMI PAPER INTERNATIONAL
www.hiromipaper.com

This local business carries a large selection of Japanese and specialty papers as well as traditional Japanese bookbinding tools.

HOLLANDER'S
www.hollanders.com

This store offers a large selection of specialty papers. You will also find all types of bookbinding tools and supplies.

MICHAELS
www.michaels.com

Michaels carries many basic craft and scrapbooking tools that work well for bookbinding. Keep an eye out for interesting string, ribbon, and embellishments.

OLFA
www.olfa.com

Here you will find the perfect cutting tools for any project.

PAPER SOURCE
www.paper-source.com

Look here for a fun selection of contemporary papers and basic bookbinding tools.

ROYALWOOD LTD.
www.royalwoodltd.com

This online source is one of the best for waxed linen thread at great prices.

TALAS
www.talasonline.com

Here you will find specialty bookbinding and conservation materials that you cannot find elsewhere.

UTRECHT
www.utrechtart.com

Utrecht is another great resource for all art materials as well as a few basic bookbinding tools.

These books are great resources for digging deeper into the nitty-gritty details of bookbinding.

Japanese Bookbinding: Instructions from a Master Craftsman
Kojiro Ikegami
Boston: Weatherhill

Non-Adhesive Binding: Books Without Paste or Glue
Keith A. Smith
Rochester, N.Y.: Keith Smith

ABOUT THE AUTHOR

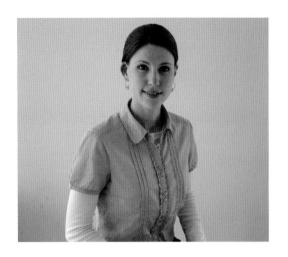

ERIN ZAMRZLA has loved making things from paper for as long as she can remember. As a design student, she took her first bookbinding class and thus began a wonderful adventure. She currently designs, paints, and binds books from her home in California. See more of her work at erinzam.com.

Special thanks to Ben and Mom. Thanks also to Jennifer Urban-Brown.

TRUMPETER BOOKS
An imprint of Shambhala Publications, Inc.
Horticultural Hall
300 Massachusetts Avenue
Boston, Massachusetts 02115
www.shambhala.com

9 8 7 6 5 4 3 2 1
First edition
Printed in China

∞This edition is printed on acid-free paper that meets the American National Standards Institute Z39.48 Standard.
♻Shambhala Publications makes every effort to print on recycled paper. For more information please visit www.shambhala.com.

Distributed in the United States by Random House, Inc., and in Canada by Random House of Canada Ltd

Designed by Daniel Urban-Brown

Library of Congress Cataloging-in-Publication Data
Zamrzla, Erin.
At home with handmade books: 28 extraordinary bookbinding projects made from ordinary and repurposed materials / Erin Zamrzla.
p.   cm.
ISBN 978-1-59030-822-6 (pbk.: alk. paper)
1. Bookbinding—Handbooks, manuals, etc. I. Title.
Z271.Z36 2011
686.3—dc22
2010033145